Brass Tacks
GRAMMAR

LYNNE GAETZ
Collège Lionel-Groulx

Prentice Hall Allyn and Bacon Canada
Scarborough, Ontario

Canadian Cataloguing in Publication Data

Gaetz, Lynne, 1960-
    Brass tacks grammar

ISBN 0-13-742503-1

1. English language - Textbooks for second language learners.* 2. English language - Grammar - Problems, exercises, etc.   I. Title.

PE1128.G327 1997   428.2'4   C96-932359-X

Prentice-Hall, Inc., Upper Saddle River, New Jersey
Prentice-Hall International (UK) Limited, London
Prentice-Hall of Australia, Pty. Limited, Sydney
Prentice-Hall Hispanoamericana, S.A., Mexico City
Prentice-Hall of India Private Limited, New Delhi
Prentice-Hall of Japan, Inc., Tokyo
Simon & Schuster Asia Private Limited, Singapore
Editora Prentice-Hall do Brasil, Ltda., Rio de Janeiro

ISBN 0-13-742503-1

Acquisitions Editor: Dominique Roberge
Developmental Editor: Marta Tomins
Production Editor: Susan James
Copy Editor: Nick Gamble
Production Coordinator: Jane Schell
Cover Design: Zena Denchick
Page Layout: Debbie Fleming

Visit the Prentice Hall Canada Web site! Send us your comments, browse our catalogues, and more. **www.phcanada.com** Or reach us through e-mail at phabinfo_pubcanada@prenhall.com

    5   BBG   01 00 99

Printed and bound in the United States.

Dedication

This book is dedicated to my students, and to my children Diego and Rebeka.

Table of Contents

Preface

Brass Tacks Grammar was made for intermediate level students of English as a Second Language (or English as a Foreign Language). It was created after I studied the typical grammatical errors made by my students at this level.

In Quebec, this book is suited for intermediate English students, and it contains all of the grammar concepts in the Quebec Ministry guidelines for that level.

Each grammar unit includes various types of exercises which can be checked against the Answer Key at the back of the book. The exercises use realistic language and common expressions. I've tried, as much as possible, to keep the explanations simple and straightforward, and the exercises generally reflect the problem areas that students have.

The tense sections are quite thorough, mainly because even advanced ESL students make tense errors. For example, many high-level ESL students consistently forget to put the *s* on verbs, and so exercises are included where students practice this concept. Each tense unit also contains exercises on the passive form of that tense.

After compiling lists of common errors made by 102-level students, I realized that a large number of students have problems with plurals. For example, students commonly put an *s* on adjectives, or they add *s* to words like *information*. A unit on plurals has been included that focuses on common plural errors.

In addition to units on the verb tenses, plurals, conditionals, and modals, this book contains exercises on punctuating (comma, semicolon and quotation marks) and capitalizing. The two final units look at common spelling errors and gallicisms.

Appendices contain descriptions of parts of speech, gerunds and infinitives, and pronouns, as well as an exercise for each concept. In addition, there are communication activities for the students to practice the structures they have learned, and a table of irregular verbs.

Each grammar concept has clear explanations, so the book could be used as a self-study manual. Any teacher who thinks that grammar is important, but doesn't have the time to explain grammar in class, could let the students work at home in this book. Grammar could also be given prescriptively, with each student doing only those chapters that relate to his or her own grammar problems.

Each section contains some "class exercises." The answers to these exercises are not in the answer key because sometimes the teacher may want to explain a concept or do an exercise with the students. These exercises could also be used as reviews or as quizzes. There are two review sections that could also be used for quizzes.

Corrections to each numbered exercise are in a separate Answer Key, available with book order. In some cases, students who work alone can do the majority of the exercises, and then correct their own answers. By doing their own correcting, students can evaluate themselves and determine whether or not they have mastered the concepts.

Now get down to *Brass Tacks*!

Acknowledgements

I would like to thank the following people for their help and support: my students, for letting me test this material with them, and the English Department at Collège Lionel-Groulx, especially Donna Canuel and Richard Pawsey. Many teachers generously tested the reading material and gave me valuable feedback, including Robin Dick, Heather Yorsten, Jean Philippe Lebonnois and Sonia Margossian. I am also indebted to Cliff Newman, Dominique Roberge, Marta Tomins, Marijke Leupen, Susan James, and Nick Gamble. I would like to thank Line Bechard, Jane Davey and Hugh Burgoyne for their encouragement, support, and suggestions. I appreciate the useful comments from Roxane Vigneault of Collège de Sherbrooke. I would like to extend a special thanks to my parents, my husband and my children, who helped keep my spirits up and who put up with my long hours on the computer.

The Present Tenses

Simple Present (General Present)

The Simple Present tense is the first verb tense that most students learn, but it is also, perhaps, the most complicated, for in this tense the student must remember to pronounce and write the final *s* on verbs that refer to third person singular subjects. What further complicates this tense is the importance of adding the auxiliaries *do* or *does* when forming some questions or negatives. If you have ever found yourself forgetting the *s* on verbs, or omitting the *do* or *does*, then study this section with particular care.

When to Use the Simple Present

Use this tense to refer to an action which is a habit or a fact.

*Fish **live** in water.* (Fact)

*Marge **visits** the dentist twice a year.* (Habit)

	Dental visit	Dental visit	Dental visit	
(Past years)				(Future years)
	January 1996	July 1996	January 1997	

Key words: always, often, usually, sometimes, seldom, rarely, never, every day, every week …

Subject-Verb Agreement

I
We ·······➤ **live** in Manitoba.
You
They

He ·······➤ **lives** in Manitoba.
She
It

1. All simple present tense verbs that refer to *one* person, place or thing (except *you* and *I*) must be conjugated with an *s* or *es*.

   Roy despis**es** coffee, but his wife, Ginger, lov**es** it.

2. Add *es* to verbs ending in *ch*, *sh*, *s*, *x*, or *z*.

   Ginger search**es** for new types of coffee, and she sometimes mix**es** brands together.

3. Don't let interrupting phrases fool you.

   That **house**, where John and Anne live, **has** many rooms.

   The new **bicycle**, which is in pieces, **includes** a set of directions.

4. *Everybody, somebody, anybody* and *nobody* are considered singular. (Also with "everyone," "everything," etc.)

   Somebody **has** my keys. Everyone **is** here. Something **is** under the rug.

5. Never add *s* to modals: *can, could, would, should, must, may, might, will, shall, ought to.*

   Sara **can come** with us but Margie **must do** her homework.

CLASS EXERCISE

Underline each subject and circle each verb (action word). Add *s* or *es* to verbs that follow third person singular subjects. Only the verb *to be* is already conjugated correctly. There are 20 verbs to conjugate in this text, not including the example.

(1) My neighbor, who is very friendly, (have) a little mutt called Sparky. As you may
            has
have guessed from the name, Sparky is one of those annoying miniature dogs. Everyone say that Sparky look like an overgrown dustbunny. He have a tiny brown mop of fur for a head, and his body, which measure about eight inches in length, look like a furry black and brown boot.

(2) Sparky is a very jumpy, nervous little dog. I'd swear that he have a cup of cappuccino every morning. Every time that little mutt catch a glimpse of me he yap, leap, shiver, shake, and, if possible, bite. If I walk on the sidewalk in front of the neighbor's house, Sparky inevitably come racing around the corner at full tilt. This is such a dumb dog that sometimes he run right past me, look momentarily confused, turn in a skid, and charge back at me. He bark, jump up and he grab my pant leg. He is more annoying than a flea on a dog's neck.

EXERCISE 1

Complete this exercise in the same way as you did the previous exercise. Conjugate 20 verbs that follow singular subjects in this text. The verb *to be* is already conjugated.

Note: *to go, to eat,* etc. are infinitives. Never add *s* to the verb that follows *to.*

(1) Ms. Murti is a very friendly woman. She have a very gentle disposition and she seem to really care about others. One of the things that everyone notice about her is the *intensity* with which she listen. When anyone talk to her, she always immediately stop whatever she is doing, she turn, and look the speaker in the eye. This ability to really listen is a quality that I admire. Ms. Murti, with her listening ability, manage to make you feel like you are the most important person in the world.

(2) Mr. Murti is not at all like his wife. He have a very gruff manner. When someone address him, he often look away, as if he can't hear that person. Everyone notice how impolite he is. Mr. Murti also interrupt people, and when he have an opinion about something, he make sure that everyone know about it. Mr. Murti, who usually ignore or insult people, actually think that he is a very pleasant fellow! Most people like Ms. Murti more than Mr. Murti.

Simple Present Tense: Negative Form

With the verb *to be*, just put *not* after the verb.

Carol is friendly.   Carol **is not** friendly. (or **isn't**)

With all other verbs, place *do* or *does* and the word *not* between the subject and the verb.

Aldo and I watch a lot of TV.   We **do not** watch a lot of TV. (or **don't**)

Mrs. Murti listens carefully.   She **does not** listen carefully. (or **doesn't**)

EXERCISE 2

Underline the verb and make it negative.

Example: The doctor <u>has</u> a nice bedside manner.   *doesn't have*

1. Ronald remembers every detail about his childhood.   _____

2. Carlos eats fried food.   _____

3. Those workers go on strike every year.   _____

4. Tomatoes are very tasty.   _____

5. April has 31 days.   _____

Simple Present Tense: Question Form

The verb *to be*: When making a question, change the word order so that *be* appears *before* the subject.

Diego **is** thirsty.   **Is** Diego thirsty?

Why **is** Diego thirsty?

With all other verbs, add the auxiliary *do* or *does* to create questions. When you add *does* to the sentence, the *s* is no longer needed on the verb.

		auxiliary		
Rebeka stretches every morning.	When	**does**	Rebeka	**stretch**?
Jerome walks in his sleep.	How often	**does**	Jerome	**walk** in his sleep?

EXERCISE 3

Create questions from the answers provided.

	Question word(s)	Auxiliary	Subject	Verb	
Example: Jerry hates dogs.	Why	does	Jerry	hate	dogs?
1. Hanna needs a lift.	What				
2. The peas are on the plate.	Where				
3. The twins usually play hockey.	When				
4. Marco often lies to people.	Why				
5. The police investigate themselves.	Why				
6. The doctor is late today.	Why				
7. The movie lasts for two hours.	How long				

Who / What Questions

When *who(m)** and *what* ask about the object of a question, an auxiliary is necessary.

The roof needs **new shingles**.   **What does** the roof need?

Tony phones **his mother** every day.   **Who (or whom) does** Tony call every day?

*Whom is rarely used in spoken English.

However, when *who* and *what* ask about the subject of a question, no auxiliary is needed.

The roof needs new shingles.   **What** needs new shingles?

Tony phones his mother every day.   **Who** phones his mother every day?

EXERCISE 4

Write questions. The answer to the question is in bold.

Example:

The boy has **peanuts** in his pocket. _What does the boy have in his pocket?_

1. The nurse has **a clipboard**. _____

2. **The nurse** has a clipboard. _____

3. **Samantha** wears second-hand clothes. _____

4. Samantha wears **second-hand clothes**. _____

5. **That house** has a large garage. _____

EXERCISE 5

Write questions. The answer to the question is in bold.

1. **Frankie** has a lot of problems at school.

_____

2. Sparky lives **in my neighbor's house**.

_____

3. Coffee gives many people **the jitters**.

_____

4. The ballet performance lasts **for two and a half hours**.

_____

5. Ms. Riffo visits the dentist **twice a year**.

_____

6. The skunks hide **under the shed** every spring.

_____

7. Chuck opens beer bottles **with his teeth**.

_____

Make the next three questions _negative_. With negative questions, attach _not_ to the auxiliary.

She doesn't own a television. _Why **doesn't** she **own** a television?_

Mark isn't home. _Why **isn't** he home?_

8. Francis and Charles aren't friendly to each other. (Why?)

_____

9. That car doesn't have any wheels. (Why?)

_____

10. Mark has no friends. (Why? Rephrase question to make a negative question.)

_____

Present Progressive

The Present Progressive is used whenever you want to indicate that an action is in progress. This tense is formed with a present form of *be*, and *ing* is added to the verb. For example, at this moment I am writing this sentence. I could not say *At this moment I write this sentence*. Sometimes students forget to add *be* before the verb (*I writing*), but it is important to form this tense correctly.

Another problem area with this tense is the correct spelling of the *ing* verb form. Should you double the last letter (*omitting*) or not (*opening*)? The rules for spelling are explained in this section.

As you know, for most rules there are exceptions. In this tense, there are certain verbs that cannot be used in the progressive form even if the action is happening now. For example, you cannot say *I am believing you now*. With the verb *believe* you must use the simple present tense even if you are talking about this moment: *I believe you now*. These *non-progressive* verbs are listed in this section, and you should remember that these verbs are non-progressive (never used in an *ing* form) in *all* progressive tenses.

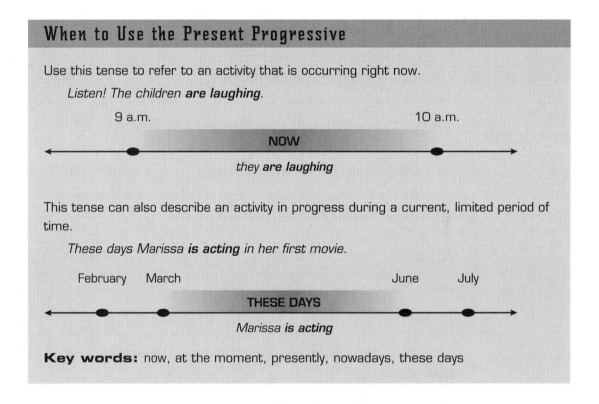

When to Use the Present Progressive

Use this tense to refer to an activity that is occurring right now.

*Listen! The children **are laughing**.*

9 a.m.   10 a.m.

NOW

*they **are laughing***

This tense can also describe an activity in progress during a current, limited period of time.

*These days Marissa **is acting** in her first movie.*

February   March   June   July

THESE DAYS

*Marissa **is acting***

Key words: now, at the moment, presently, nowadays, these days

Present Progressive Tense: Question Form

Be acts as an auxiliary and goes before the subject.

Rick (is) climbing a ladder.   *Why (is) Rick climbing a ladder?*

Present Progressive Tense: Negative Form

Place *not* after the verb *be*.

Alf is studying for his test.   Alf **is not (isn't)** *studying for his test.*

CLASS EXERCISE

Make *a statement*, *a question*, and *a negative sentence* out of the words in parentheses. Use either the simple present or the present progressive tense.

Example: (Carol / bite her lip / now)   *She's biting her lip now.*
Is she biting her lip now?
She isn't biting her lip now.

1. (the politician / lie / everyday) _____

_____

_____

2. (your sister / cut her toenails / now) _____

_____

_____

3. (Mr. Ed / have / long dirty hair) _____

_____

_____

4. (Terri / knock / on the door) _____

_____

_____

5. (your brother / have a temper tantrum / now) _____

_____

_____

6. (most people / have / a television) _____

_____

_____

7. (you / need a passport / to visit Mexico) _____

_____

_____

8. (the children / understand / Spanish) _____

_____

_____

Non-Progressive Verbs

These verbs cannot be used in the progressive tense.

Perception verbs	Preference verbs	State verbs
see	like	know
hear	love	think (opinion)
feel	hate	mean
taste	care	suppose
smell	prefer	understand
look (meaning "appear")	want	believe
seem	wish	realize
	desire	own / belong

Some of these verbs can be used in the present progressive tense when they describe a process or action.

Compare:

I am looking at you.   *That dinner looks good!*

He is seeing Rosa. (meaning: dating)   *Louis sees really well without glasses.*

EXERCISE 6

Complete the sentences using the simple present or the present progressive. Use the Present Progressive (*be ...ing*) when the action is in progress now, or for this period of time.

1. I (know) _____ Ziggy Brown. (you, know) _____ him? He (act, sometimes) _____ in the theater with my brother. I (think) _____ they (rehearse) _____ for a show right now.

2. This tea (smell) _____ good. I (like) _____ strong tea, but my husband, Ed, (drink, not) _____ it. He (think) _____ that caffeine gives him the jitters. Now he (relax) _____ in front of the TV set. He (watch) _____ a football game. Sometimes Ed (act) _____ like a real couch potato. I (like, not) _____ to watch TV.

3. At the moment my brother (live) _____ in Toronto. He (look) _____ for a job anywhere in Canada. My parents were born in Calgary and they (live, still) _____ in Alberta. My younger sister (stay) _____ with my parents temporarily until she gets accepted at a university. She (wait) _____ for news from one of Canada's universities. As for me, I (live) _____ in Halifax. I am a computer programmer, but I (work, not) _____ right now.

Spelling of ing Verb Forms

1. When verbs end in *y*, always keep the *y* and add *ing*.

try – *trying*   play – *playing*

2. Double the *last* letter of one-syllable verbs that end with a consonant-vowel-consonant combination.

run – *running*   stop – *stopping*

Exceptions: *Quit* (two vowels) becomes *quitting*.

3. Double the last letter of longer verbs when they end in a *stressed* consonant-vowel-consonant combination.

re**fer** – *referring*   **o**pen – *opening*

(Second syllable is stressed,   (First syllable is stressed,
so double the last letter.)   so do not double the last letter.)

Exceptions: Never double the last letter of verbs ending in *w* or *x*.

EXERCISE 7

Write the present participle (*ing* form) in the space provided.

1. come _____   **6.** happen _____

2. open _____   **7.** occur _____

3. tip _____   **8.** rain _____

4. shop _____   **9.** remain _____

5. write _____   **10.** omit _____

CLASS EXERCISE

Fill in the blanks with the simple present tense or the present progressive tense.

1. What (happen) _____ these days? I (refer) _____
to the violence in the world. Humans (kill) _____ each other, at
this moment, in every country on the planet.

2. Alice (sit, usually) _____ in the back row of movie theaters but
today she (sit) _____ in the front row. She (wear, not)
_____ her glasses today, so she (see, not) _____
well. Today I (sit, also) _____ near the front.

3. At the moment Kevin (stare) _____ out his window. He
sees the children (shout) _____ and some trucks (honk)

_____ their horns. A thief (rob) _____

the corner store. The store's alarm system (wail) _____ .

I (hear, not) _____ any traffic and I (smell, not)

_____ any pollution because I live in the countryside.

4. Clara (knit) _____ a sweater for her son. Many people

(know, not) _____ how to knit. (your father,

know) _____ how to knit?

5. Karen (see) _____ someone these days. I (know)

_____ it! Look at her over there! At this moment she (walk)

_____ around like she is on cloud nine. Hey! (you, listen)

_____ to me right now?

When to Use Apostrophes

Use apostrophes:

1. to join a subject and verb together.   _**We're** late. **There's** nothing to eat._

2. to join an auxiliary with _not_.   _I **can't** come. They **aren't** very friendly._

3. to indicate possession.   _That is **Simon's** car. **Ross's** computer is new._

Never use an apostrophe before the **s** at the end of a verb.

   Incorrect: _Mother make's_

   Correct: _Mother makes_

EXERCISE 8

Add apostrophes where necessary.

1. Hannas father, Fred, works for General Motors, but Freds taking a vacation right now.

2. The Maliks live near the mines, but the Girards home is near the lake.

3. Mr. Maliks son needs work now, but he doesnt want to work in the mines.

4. He wants to work at his uncles company, but right now there arent any jobs available.

5. Mr. Girards daughter works at Smiths Appliances, but she doesnt want to stay there.

EXERCISE 9

Underline and correct the errors in the following present tense sentences. If the sentence is correct, write *C* in the space provided.

1. Nobody deserve to suffer through a long and painful illness.   _____

2. Barney is very athletic and he is going to the gym every second day.   _____

3. Alice and Dan eats dinner together every Friday night.   _____

4. Simon isn't understanding you very well, so please speak more slowly.   _____

5. Melanie, who work's with me, is very ill right now.   _____

6. Why is Clara is sitting all alone over there?   _____

7. The children are so quiet! I think they are relaxing in the back yard.   _____

8. Sorry, but Mary is a person who don't like to eat meat.   _____

9. Do anybody want more coffee?   _____

10. Laura is the type of person who always judge a book by its cover.   _____

CLASS EXERCISE

The present tense verbs in this text are in *italics*. Some of the verbs are spelled and used correctly, but others have errors. Correct any verb errors. After the example, there are 12 errors.

(1) Right now I *siting* (am sitting) on my back porch, and I *am watching* an amazing event that *is occuring* before my eyes. The mountains, which *form's* a wall on the horizon, *stand* majestically, and the clouds *are* in the shape of an arch. All of the clouds above the arch *are* thick and gray, and the sky inside the arch *is* clear blue. The chinook winds *are comming* with their warm, balmy air and I *am enjoiing* every minute of it.

(2) Although I left this town many years ago, I *am* extremely happy to be back. The big sky *is* something that a prairie person never *forget*. Anyone who *live* near here *know* what I'm talking about. The flat, golden prairies *stretch* for miles, and the sky *seems* infinite in its grandeur. Sometimes, on days when everyone *are busy walking, working, writting letters, and basically living* an ordinary existence, the sky suddenly *lights* up with flashes of color that *seems* to reflect from the earth. The northern lights *are* breathtaking, the chinook arches *are* glorious, and even the clear blue sky *attract* people's attention. Here, on the edge of the prairies, everyone always *studys* the sky.

Present Tenses in the Passive Voice

A sentence is *active* when the subject of the sentence does the action, and *passive* when the subject of the sentence receives the action. Passive voice should not be overused, and is effective mainly when the result of the action is more important than who performed the action.

1. In the *simple present* tense, the passive voice is formed with *be* (am / is / are) + the past participle. (See the verb list at the end of this book.)

Active	Passive
*Many students **use** computers.*	*Computers **are used** by many students.*
Students do the action.	The subject (*computers*) is acted on by the students.

2. In the *present progressive* tense, the passive voice is formed with the present progressive form of *be* (am being / is being / are being) + the past participle.

Active	Passive
*Right now Julie **is using** the printer.*	*The printer **is being used**. [by Julie]**

*The "*by* ... " phrase is not always necessary.

EXERCISE 10

Change the following sentences from the active to the passive voice. The verb to be changed is in italics.

Example: My son *is washing* the kitchen floor.

   The kitchen floor is being washed by my son.

1. General Motors *produces* many cars.

_____

2. As we speak, the workers *are producing* over forty cars.

_____

3. Right now the B team *is making* a car door.

_____

4. People in this area also *create* many other products.

_____

5. People on assembly lines *manufacture* many useful products.

_____

6. Unfortunately, machines *are replacing* human workers these days.

_____

2 The Past Tenses

The past tenses in English do not contain complexities like *s* on third person singular verbs. Only the verb *be* has two past forms (*was* and *were*). In fact, in some respects the past tense is relatively simple: the same verb form (such as *looked*) can be used with all persons.

However, this tense is complicated because of the irregular verb forms that must be memorized. There is a list of common irregular past tense verbs at the back of this book. The Simple Past, like the Simple Present, also requires an auxiliary (*did*) in most question and negative forms.

Simple Past

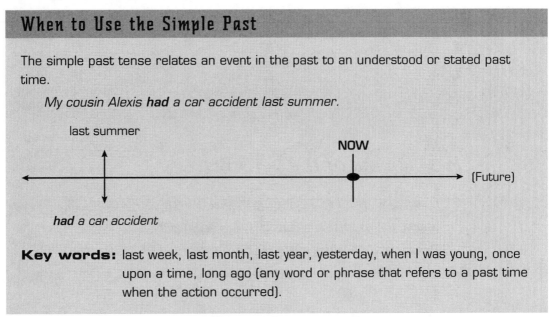

When to Use the Simple Past

The simple past tense relates an event in the past to an understood or stated past time.

*My cousin Alexis **had** a car accident last summer.*

last summer

NOW

(Future)

***had** a car accident*

Key words: last week, last month, last year, yesterday, when I was young, once upon a time, long ago (any word or phrase that refers to a past time when the action occurred).

Spelling of Regular Past Tense Verbs

There are both regular and irregular past tense verbs. Regular verbs take *ed* and generally do not appear in verb lists, such as the one at the back of this book, because of their standard form.

1a. Double the *last* letter of one-syllable verbs that end in a consonant-vowel-consonant combination.

stop – *stopped*   jog – *jogged*

1b. Double the last letter of longer verbs when they end in a *stressed* consonant-vowel-consonant combination.

pre**fer** – *preferred*   **o**pen – *opened*
(Second syllable is stressed,   (First syllable is stressed,
so double the last letter)   so do not double the last letter)

2a. When verbs end in consonant-*y*, change the *y* to *i* and add *ed*.

fry – *fried*   apply – *applied*

2b. When verbs end in vowel-*y*, usually keep the *y*.

play – *played*   **Exception:** pay – *paid*

EXERCISE 1

Write the *ed* form of these regular verbs.

1. believe _____	**6.** remain _____	**11.** rain _____
2. prefer _____	**7.** jog _____	**12.** try _____
3. rely _____	**8.** offer _____	**13.** plan _____
4. marry _____	**9.** hope _____	**14.** die _____
5. happen _____	**10.** tip _____	**15.** open _____

Past Forms of the Verb Be

1. Use *was* with *I, he, she* and *it*. Use *were* with *you, we* and *they*.

Marla, *the girl with the red hair,* **was** *very flighty.*

Patrick and Alice were *late for class yesterday.*

2. With "dummy" subjects like *there*, make sure that your verb agrees with the following nouns.

There **was** *a tiny ink* **stain** *on my sweater.*

There **were** *several ink* **stains** *on his sleeve.*

EXERCISE 2

Fill in the blanks with the simple past verb forms.

1. When I (be) _____ a child, I (visit) _____ my
grandmother every summer. Granny Maud (have) _____ the
unusual habit of frequently moving, so whenever we (look) _____
for her home, we had to get the new address from one of my uncles.

2. Although Granny (move) _____ often, she was very consistent in
one way: her homes always (contain) _____ a special glassed-off
room. This salon, where the plastic-covered furniture (be) _____
kept, (be) _____ always off-limits to the grandchildren.

3. As children we often (press) _____ our noses against the glass to
look at the fancy furniture in the salon. There (be) _____ always
many statues, elaborately framed photos and unusual knickknacks. One of the
items that I especially (enjoy) _____ (be) _____ a
tiny porcelain clock. Inside the decorated clock (be) _____ two tiny
girls sitting on a tiny swing. As each second (tick) _____ the tiny
girls swung like a pendulum.

4. Unfortunately I rarely (try) _____ to tell my granny how much I
loved her. The day that my granny (stop) _____ breathing, it
(occur) _____ to me that I really (miss) _____ her.

Irregular Verbs

EXERCISE 3

Do you know the past forms of these irregular verbs? Write the past tense form in the
space provided.

1. keep _____	**6.** sink _____	**11.** sleep _____
2. write _____	**7.** think _____	**12.** buy _____
3. bring _____	**8.** feel _____	**13.** ring _____
4. fall _____	**9.** sell _____	**14.** hang _____
5. spend _____	**10.** fight _____	**15.** shake _____

Past Tense: Question Form

Verb Be

When making a question, change the word order so that the verb *be* appears before the subject.

They (were) late.　　　　　　(Were) they late?

　　　　　　　　　　　　　　Why **were** they late?

All Other Verbs

With all other verbs, add the auxiliary *did* to create questions. When you add *did* to the sentence, you no longer need to keep the verb in the past tense. *Did* makes the question a past tense question.

　　　　　　　　　　　　　　　　　　　　　　auxiliary

Ralph married Alice in 1958.　　*When* **did** *Ralph* **marry** *Alice?*

Marvin drank too much beer.　　*Why* **did** *Marvin* **drink** *all of the beer?*

When *who* or *what* ask about the *subject* of a question, no *did* is required.

Who drank too much beer?　　*Marvin drank too much beer.*

Past Tense: Negative Form

Verb Be

Place *not* after the verb *be*.

They were **not** *late.*

All Other Verbs

Place *not* after the auxiliary.

Ralph **did not** *marry Alice in 1958.*

EXERCISE 4

Make questions from the following sentences. The answer is in bold.

Example: Becky ate **the grapes**.　　*What did Becky eat?*

1. Marco called **Alicia** yesterday.

_____

2. **Marco** called Alicia yesterday.

_____

3. Sam cut her toenails **because they were too long**.

_____

4. Ricardo and Mia sang **"La Bamba"** at the festival.

_____

5. Mia sang in a choir **for twelve years**.

_____

6. Robert did the laundry **last Saturday**.

_____

7. Ricky went to a hockey game **yesterday**.

_____

8. The farm was **four kilometers** from the nearest phone.

_____

9. Her dead dog's name was **Lucky**.

_____

10. Moe gave the bookie **fifty dollars** yesterday.

_____

11. Denis made **blueberry muffins** last weekend.

_____

12. Bert swam **across the lake** last summer.

_____

EXERCISE 5

In the following sentences, underline the verb(s) and change them to the past tense.

	Now	**In 1974**
	Example: Maurice <u>keeps</u> his valuables in a safe.	_kept_
1.	Mrs. Romanov teaches children how to speak Russian.	_____
2.	Anton chooses to learn German also.	_____
3.	Anton writes, but doesn't speak, German.	_____
4.	Anton's sister Katya flies a single-engine plane.	_____
5.	Anton doesn't know how to fly a plane.	_____
6.	Katya spends a lot of time in the air.	_____
7.	Mrs. Romanov shakes when she goes into an airplane.	_____
8.	She is afraid of heights.	_____
9.	Katya pays for her own flying lessons.	_____
10.	By paying for her lessons, Katya proves that she is independent.	_____

When Not *to Use the Past Verb Form*

Never use the past verb form:

1. after *to* in infinitive forms.

Incorrect: *The children needed to spoke with us.*

Correct: *The children needed **to speak** with us.*

2. after *did. Did* makes a sentence past tense, and the following verb must be in the present form.

Incorrect: *Mother didn't told us why you were late.*

Correct: *Mother **didn't tell** us why you were late.*

CLASS EXERCISE

Correct the verb errors in the following sentences. There is one error per sentence.

1. Last weekend I really wanted to saw that rock band, but the tickets were too expensive.

2. When I was a child, there was rules, and we had to follow them.

3. The insects didn't survived the pesticide spraying.

4. My teacher, Ms. Ritchie, tought me how to play the piano.

5. A long time ago a king made a tournament to knew who would get the throne.

6. Tweetie Bird tought he saw a putty cat a moment ago.

7. Did he saw a cat?

8. What happenned when the fight was over?

9. There was over forty people at the wedding reception.

10. The legendary King Arthur wanted to found a queen.

Avoiding Tense Shifts

If you start to tell a story, do not shift tenses unless the time frame really does change.

*Jerry **left** his apartment and Kramer **enters** moments later.*

(The tense incorrectly shifts from the past to the present.)

EXERCISE 6

In the following exercise, correct any tense shifts. In the past tense, use *would* instead of *will*.

(1) Some people really want to be alone and preferred to spend most of their time in solitary activities. Joan, a girl that I went to school with, was really like that. Every day when we went outside for recess, Joan stays inside. When the other kids played with skipping ropes and marbles, Joan will sit quietly in a corner of the schoolyard and read a book. Sometimes I asked Joan to play with us but she never wants to.

(2) Even though she didn't have any friends at school, she never seems lonely. She will smile to herself as she did her solitary activities. I met Joan many years later, when I was about nineteen, on an airplane. She told me that she was going to France to study mime. She seemed so friendly and happy. We sat together on the flight and talk for hours.

Past Progressive

The Past Progressive is formed with the past forms of the verb *be* (*was*, *were*) and the *ing* verb form. This tense is sometimes overused by second language learners. For example, French speakers sometimes incorrectly translate the *imparfait* into the past progressive. Only use the past progressive tense when you want to specify that one action was in progress when another action occurred, or when you want to indicate that a past action was in progress at a specific past time.

For example, it is incorrect to say *Yesterday I was watching TV*. Unless you spent the entire day in front of the television, such a sentence doesn't make sense. It would be more appropriate in this case to use the simple past, and say *Yesterday I watched TV*. Now the sentence just means that at some point yesterday you watched TV, but you probably did many other things as well.

Only use the past progressive in the following two ways. You could say *Yesterday at noon I was watching TV*. In this sentence you clarify that the past action was in progress at a specific time. You could also say *Yesterday while I was watching TV the power went out*, indicating that the past action was in progress when another action occurred.

Keep in mind that some verbs are non-progressive, and the list in Chapter 1 also applies to past progressive verbs. For example, you cannot say *I was understanding* because *understand* cannot be used in the progressive form.

When to Use the Past Progressive

Use the past progressive to:

1. describe an action that was in progress when another action interrupted it.

*Last Friday we **were watching** TV when Anne fainted.*

NOW

we ***were watching*** *TV*

Interruption: *Anne fainted*

2. describe an action that was in progress at a specific, indicated time.

*Yesterday evening at 8 p.m. I **was eating** supper.*

NOW

*I **was eating** supper*

Precise time: *8 p.m.*

3. describe two actions that were continuing at the same time.

Yesterday, while I **was setting** the table, my sister **was resting** on the sofa.*
*Use the past progressive after *while*.

EXERCISE 7

Fill in the blanks with the simple past or the past progressive tense.

1. During my childhood, I (understand, not) _____ the value of education.

2. Yesterday evening, Steve (read) _____ a book in the bathroom when I (yell) _____ that supper was ready.

3. The students (discuss) _____ the issue when Evan suddenly (faint) _____ . In the past, my old teacher often (discuss) _____ that issue.

4. The bride (walk) _____ up the aisle when she (slip) _____ on a banana peel. (You, see) _____ the bride slip on the banana peel? It was very funny!

5. I really had to complain to the landlord. Last night, while I (try) _____ to sleep, my downstairs neighbour (play) _____ his saxophone!

6. On March 1, at the time of the murder, I (babysit) _____ my sister's children in the park. I (see, not) _____ or (hear) _____ a thing.

CLASS EXERCISE

Put either the simple past or the past progressive verb form in the spaces provided.
(20 spaces)

1. My grandfather (come) _____ to Canada in 1924. He

(leave) _____ Russia, and he (ride)

_____ across Europe on the railroad. His family then

(board) _____ a ship headed to America. They (have)

_____ almost no possessions, but my grandfather had a

gold wristwatch that his uncle had given him.

2. As the boat (leave) _____ France, my grandfather (lean)

_____ on the rail to watch the receding shore. While he

(bend) _____ over to look at the water, the gold watch

(slip) _____ from his wrist and (fall)

_____ into the ocean.

3. While the ship (cross) _____ the ocean, my grandfather

(fall) _____ ill. He (have) _____ a

fever, and his parents (be, not) _____ sure that my

grandfather would survive. For several hours he (lose) _____

consciousness. A large storm (hit) _____ while the boat

(approach) _____ the Canadian shore. While the ship

(toss) _____ and (turn) _____ on

the waves, my grandfather (regain) _____ consciousness.

Past Tenses in the Passive Voice

The past tense, like the present tense, has a passive voice form.

1. In the simple past, the passive voice is formed with the past form of *be* (was /
were) + the past participle.

Active	Passive
*Workers from China **made** that coat.*	*That coat **was made** in China. (by workers)*

2. In the past progressive, the passive voice is formed with the past progressive form
of *be* (was being / were being) + the past participle.

Active	Passive
*At 8 p.m., John **was using** the machine.*	*At 8 p.m., the machine **was being used**. (by John)*

EXERCISE 8

Determine if the following sentences are active or passive. Underline the verb and write *P* (Passive) or *A* (Active) in the space provided.

1. Boots are sold at that store.   _____

2. I bought a nice pair of leather boots there last Tuesday.   _____

3. The boots were made in Mexico.   _____

4. Now I am wearing the boots.   _____

5. At work I was asked about the boots.   _____

CLASS EXERCISE

Fill in the blanks with the past tense form in either the active or the passive voice.

1. A few years ago a great chess-playing computer (develop) _____ by an American company. The chess champion, Gary Kasparov, (challenge) _____ to a match by the computer company. The company (want) _____ to see if their computer, "Deep Blue," could beat a human opponent.

2. Just before his fortieth move, Kasparov (pick) _____ up his watch and (put) _____ it on. A ripple of laughter (hear) _____ from the crowd. The "watch" manoeuvre (mean) _____ that Kasparov (feel) _____ confident that the game was his.

3. Many people (surprise) _____ by the strong performance of the computer, but they (feel) _____ relieved that humanity's superiority over machines was still intact. After winning the game, Kasparov (give) _____ a standing ovation by the crowd.

The Present Perfect Tenses

What can complicate second-language learning is the fact that some languages have tenses that don't exist in other languages. For example, English has a tense called the Present Perfect, but no such tense exists in French.

If you listen to English people speak, you will notice that this tense is very common, and is used in many circumstances. For example, the following paragraph is one side of a typical telephone call. Can you identify the present perfect tense in this example?

> I haven't seen you for a while. Have you done anything interesting lately? Have you seen any good movies? Have you gone to any good plays? I haven't been out of the house for two weeks, because I've had a terrible cold. On top of that, my sister has been in town for the last week, and she hasn't had time to see me yet.

This tense is always formed with an auxiliary (*have* or *has*) and the past participle. You can never use the simple past verb form with this tense. For example, you cannot say *I have already ate*. You must use the past participle *eaten* in order to form the correct sentence, *I have already eaten*. A list of irregular past participles is at the back of this book.

In order to use this tense properly, it is useful to understand why this tense is being used. The box below illustrates the two completely different situations in which this tense is needed.

Present Perfect

The present perfect is formed with *have* or *has* and the past participle.

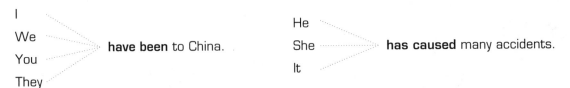

I
We
You
They
→ **have been** to China.

He
She
It
→ **has caused** many accidents.

When to Use the Present Perfect

There are two very distinct ways to use this tense:

1. Past Action Continues to the Present

Example: *Carmen **has lived** in Red Deer since 1991.*

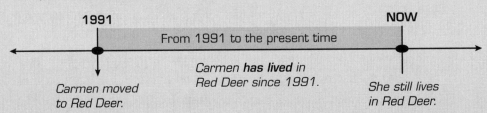

1991

From 1991 to the present time

*Carmen **has lived** in Red Deer since 1991.*

NOW

Carmen moved to Red Deer.

She still lives in Red Deer.

Key words: never, ever, not ... yet, so far, up to now (from past to present time), since, for (period of time up to the present)

2. Past time(s) unknown

Example: *Charlie **has seen** the movie <u>Casablanca</u>. He **has seen** it three times.*

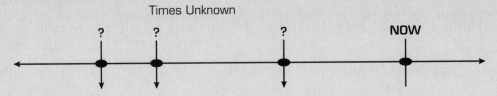

Times Unknown

?   ?   ?   **NOW**

*Charlie **has seen** the movie three times.*

Key words: already, once, twice, three times, many times... (before now)

You can also use the present perfect to describe recent events, with words like *recently, just, lately.*

EXERCISE 1

Subject and verb agreement review: circle the verb that should be used with the subject.

 1. Both Rebeka and Diego *(is / are)* ready to leave now.

 2. Who among us *(is / are)* best able to do the job?

 3. There *(is / are)* many adult students in the college.

 4. Everybody in the family *(is / are)* coming to the reunion.

 5. Mathematics *(was / were)* one of his favorite subjects. ·

 6. She's the type of person who *(lie / lies)* constantly.

 7. Where *(is / are)* your hat and gloves?

 8. Everyone in this room *(have / has)* to take responsibility for this mess.

 9. Languages *(has / have)* been taught here for many years.

10. The furniture *(was / were)* stored in the basement locker.

11. Standing in front of the crowd *(was / were)* Stuart and his brother.

12. No one really *(expect / expects)* to win the prize.

13. The information that she gave me *(was / were)* very interesting and relevant.

14. A dictionary and a verb list *(is / are)* necessary in order to complete the test.

15. *(Has / Have)* anybody seen my car keys?

Present Perfect Tense: Question Form

Place the auxiliary *have* or *has* before the subject.

We (have) known him for ten years.   (Have) we **known** him for ten years?

How long **have** we **known** him?

Present Perfect Tense: Negative Form

Place *not* after the auxiliary *have*.

She has been to China.   She has **not** been to China.

Practice with the Present Perfect

Exercises 2 to 5 practice using the *present perfect where past action continues to the present*.

EXERCISE 2

Fill in the blanks using the present perfect tense only. Key words that indicate when the present perfect is used are in bold.

Dear Ginger,

How (you, be) _____ **lately**? I (miss) _____ you so much **since you went away**. (You, see) _____ any of your old friends **yet**? (You, go) _____ to any of your old haunts **yet**? Nothing (be) _____ the same here **since you left**. I (be, not) _____ able to get you out of my mind! I (walk) _____ all over town looking for faces that remind me of you, but I (find, not) _____ anybody, **yet**, who has red hair like yours. **In my life** I (never, see) _____ green eyes as lovely as yours. **So far**, you are the only woman that I (love, **ever**) _____ . Please come back soon. I know that you (be, not) _____ away **for long**, but I can't take it anymore. I need you.

Love Eddy

When to Use *For, Since,* and *Ago*

Since refers to a specific time in the past when the action began.

    *Lois has worked at IBM **since** 1994.*

For refers to the amount of time that the action lasts. *For* can be used in other tenses.

Compare: *Clark worked at IBM **for** three years right after university.*

            *Lois has worked at IBM **for** three years.*

            *Next summer, Suki will visit me **for** three weeks.*

Ago refers to a time in the past when a completed action occurred.

    *Clark left IBM 20 years **ago**.*

EXERCISE 3

Fill in the blanks with *since, for,* or *ago.*

1. She has been asleep _____ hours.

2. Don't call him. He left two days _____ .

3. Clara has been acting that way _____ ages.

4. Mark hasn't washed his hair _____ last weekend.

5. Those children have had lice _____ several months.

6. I've lived in that house _____ I was a little kid.

7. A long time _____ an evil giant climbed down the beanstalk.

8. She's been ill ever _____ she had her tonsils out.

9. My uncle's had a cold _____ at least two weeks.

10. He hasn't called me _____ we graduated from high school.

EXERCISE 4

In the following exercise fill in the blanks with the simple past or present perfect tense.

1. Chandra and Jane (get) _____ engaged **three weeks ago**. They (be) _____ engaged **for three weeks**. They (be) _____ engaged **since the party**.

2. Aldo (come) _____ to Canada from Italy three months ago. Aldo (be) _____ in Canada for a few months.

3. Mr. and Mrs. Canuel (meet) _____ many years ago. They (know) _____ each other for over twenty years.

4. We (enter) _____ this class half an hour ago. We (be) _____ in this class for half an hour. We (be) _____ in our seats since 12:30.

EXERCISE 5

Proofread, and correct the error(s) in the following sentences. Highlight key words to help you decide the appropriate verb tense (key words are in bold in questions 1 and 2).

1. **Yesterday** I was waiting for my turn to use the banking machine when I've seen a robbery.

2. That is truly the best show that I've **ever** saw.

3. They have fought over money since many years.

4. Up to now, my parents have always treat me very well.

5. She is the sweetest child that I ever seen.

6. I'm sorry but I didn't finish my homework yet.

7. Walter has graduated from university last June.

8. Margaret is a secretary for twenty years.

9. I have seen Karen's new baby two weeks ago.

10. Since her remarriage Sally has try to become friends with her stepdaughter.

CLASS EXERCISE

Use either the present perfect or the simple past tense in the following sentences. Key words or phrases are in bold in number 1.

1. Judy (be) _____ in this town **for almost twenty years**. I (move) _____ here **one year ago**. I (meet) _____ Judy in an art class that I (take) _____ **last summer**. **When the course was over**, I (invite) _____ Judy for a coffee. We (be) _____ friends **ever since**.

2. My landlord, Mr. Selzer, knows Judy. He (know) _____ Judy for many years. He (teach) _____ Judy when she was in high school. She (be) _____ a very bad student, according to Mr. Selzer. Judy often (miss) _____ her math class when she was in high school.

3. Judy (see, not) _____ Mr. Selzer for many years. She never comes to my apartment building because she doesn't want to see her old math teacher. Last week, we (meet) _____ at the Cafe Santropol. After drinking some coffee, we (go) _____ to the Palace Theater.

4. At first, I (like, not) _____ this town but now that I (be) _____ here for one year, I (learn) _____ to love this place.

Present Perfect vs. Simple Past

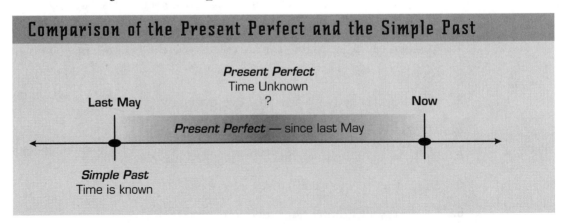

Present perfect tense is used:

1. when an action that began in the past continues to the present and possibly to the future.

*I **have been** in this seat for two hours.*

2. to talk about a completed past action (or actions) when we don't know or care about the time that the action occurred.

*Franz **has studied** over thirty types of poisonous plants.*

Simple past tense is used:

1. when an action is over and the time that the action occurred is known.

*Twenty years ago, Antonio **met** his wife Alicia.*

2. if the event happened at an understood time in the past.

***Did** you **put** away the bath towel?*
(Even if the time is not stated, if your mother asks you this question and both you and she are aware that you had a bath ten minutes earlier, then the past tense is used.)

3. if you are telling a story about an event that occurred completely in the past.

*Once upon a time, a small boy **lost** his way in the forest. Suddenly a...*

*When I was in Miami, I **saw** a shark the size of a small boat! The shark...*

Exercises 6 to 8 practice using the *present perfect where the past time is unknown.*

EXERCISE 6

Fill in the blanks with either the present perfect tense or the simple past tense.

1. Alfred (marry) _____ many women. He (marry) _____ Rosa in 1992.

2. Rosa (eat) _____ in every restaurant on Fifth Avenue. Rosa and I (eat) _____ at The Blue Lagoon Restaurant last New Year's Eve.

3. My brother (meet) _____ several famous people. My brother (meet) _____ Bob Dylan at a theater in 1984.

4. Lately my girlfriend and I (have) _____ trouble communicating. Just last week my girlfriend (throw) _____ a pillow at me.

5. Daniel and Julia (have) _____ at least twenty fights. Daniel is a big drinker. He (try) _____ to quit drinking several times. At the moment he doesn't drink. He (be) _____ on the wagon for about three weeks.

6. Mr. and Mrs. Arnold (be) _____ to New York twice. (you, think, ever) _____ about visiting New York?

7. I think that Robin (act) _____ in over fifteen movies. I (go) _____ to his latest movie last Thursday. I read that he (appear) _____ in several television shows.

EXERCISE 7

Fill in the blanks with either the present perfect tense, the simple past tense, or the past progressive tense.

1. Kevin (be) _____ a working artist for over ten years, but he (be, never) _____ able to support himself by selling his paintings. He (produce) _____ a lot of excellent work, and he (exhibit) _____ in several galleries in both Montreal and New York.

2. Kevin (receive) _____ a scholarship to study at an art college in Vancouver two years ago. As soon as he (get) _____ the money, he immediately (fly) _____ to Vancouver. After his arrival, while he (search) _____ for a cheap apartment, he (meet) _____ a girl called Holly. Holly (find) _____ a room for Kevin in the rooming house where she lives. Kevin (live) _____ in that rooming house ever since.

3. I (meet, never) _____ Holly. According to Kevin, Holly has skin the color of macaroni, hair the color of golden honey, and she is from a tiny town called Rattlesnake Hill. One day last year Kevin (notice) _____ a photograph on Terry's dresser. In the photo, Holly (stand) _____ next to a man. The man's muscled, tattooed arm (be) _____ around Holly.

4. Kevin (ask) _____ Holly who the man was. Holly (tell) _____ Kevin that the man is her brother, Frank. Apparently Frank is the mayor of Rattlesnake Hill. Frank (be) _____ the mayor of that town for several years. About four years ago, a doctor (remove) _____ Frank's tattoo with a laser.

EXERCISE 8

Write questions for the following answers using the appropriate tense. The answer to the question is in bold.

    Example: Dorothy went to Oz **to see the Wizard.**

        Why did Dorothy go to Oz?

1. Kathy has gained **15 pounds.**

_____

2. They slaughtered the pig **because they were hungry.**

_____

3. Rajiv has been to Malaysia **four times.**

_____

4. My brother owes me **two hundred dollars.**

_____

5. Jerry left the army in 1979. He stayed in the army **for three years.**

_____

6. Santiago is in the army. He has been in the army **for two years.**

_____

7. Karen quit smoking **eight years ago.**

_____

8. Ralph has smoked cigars **for thirty years.**

_____

CLASS EXERCISE

Proofread and correct the errors in the following sentences. If the sentence is correct, write *C* beside it. The first sentence has been corrected for you.

    Example: Janice Joplin (has) died in 1971.

        (Time is known so past tense must be used.)

1. Have you ever watch the show called *Mr. Bean?*

2. Since Kurt's death, his widow Courtney has a lot of trouble dealing with solitude.

3. When my mother was a child, she lived on a farm.

4. My brother Terry, who is the oldest child in my family, have been to NASA.

5. Last winter Tony has tried to get a better job.

6. So far this year, she has performed in two plays!

7. I must admit that I never seen a film as uplifting as *It's a Wonderful Life.*

8. I'm sorry, but you can't borrow that book. I haven't finished reading it yet.

9. I don't want to go to that movie with you because I already saw that film.

10. Once upon a time Snow White has met seven little dwarfs.

Present Perfect in the Passive Voice

You have seen that the passive voice is always formed with *be* and the past participle.

The present perfect is formed with *has* or *have* + *be* (*been*) + the past participle.

Active	Passive
Uri **has made** *many sales.*	*Many sales* **have been made** *(by Uri)*

EXERCISE 9

In the space below each sentence, identify the verb tense. Then change the active voice to the passive voice.

Example:

Active	**Passive**
The mice eat cheese every day.	*Cheese* **is eaten** *by the mice every day.*
Simple present tense	

1. Malaysian trees produce rubber.

_____

Rubber _____ by Malaysian trees.

2. Fred is using the computer.

_____

The computer _____ by Fred.

3. Inca Leathers made those belts.

_____

Those belts _____ by Inca Leathers.

4. At 10 p.m. John was fixing my car.

_____

At 10 p.m. my car _____ (by John).

5. Alberta has exported wheat for years.

_____

Wheat _____ by Alberta for years.

EXERCISE 10

Fill in the blanks with the correct tense in either the active or the passive voice.

1. In my father's home town, there are very few industries. The largest factory in town is the Winn Glass Factory. In fact, glass (produce) _____ by that company for over forty years. Every year, many of the local youth (hire) _____ by that factory when they finish high school.

2. My uncle (work) _____ at that company for over thirty years. Over the last few years production (cut) _____ to less than half of what it once was, so many local employees (lose) _____ their jobs. The union (go) _____ on strike several times since the factory opened.

CLASS EXERCISE

Continue filling in the blanks with the active or passive voice.

1. Sometimes accidents happen at the factory. Every day the glass (heat) _____ to such a high temperature that accidents can, and do, occur. My cousin (injure) _____ last March in a factory accident. On a regular basis all of the employees (tell) _____ by the bosses to sleep well and avoid alcohol before long shifts, but many of the employees (listen, not) _____ . Last March the bosses (ask) _____ by the employees' union to stay out the workers' private lives.

2. Since the recession, many "golden handshakes" (give) _____ to senior employees because the company is downsizing. Last June my aunt (ask) _____ my uncle to accept the golden handshake, but my uncle (want, not) _____ to retire at that time.

Present Perfect Progressive

The Present Perfect Progressive indicates that an action has been in progress from a past time up to the present.

It is formed with *have been* or *has been* + the *ing* form. The non-progressive verb list in Chapter 1 applies to this tense as it does to all progressive tenses. For example, you cannot say *I have been hating pizza for years* because *hate* is a non-progressive verb, and cannot be used in the *ing* form.

When to Use the Present Perfect Progressive

Use the present perfect progressive to emphasize the duration of an incomplete activity.

> I **have been driving** this car for eight hours.

The activity is still in progress, and the length of time spent doing the unpleasant chore is stressed.

You can also use the present perfect progressive to indicate that the results of an action are still visible.

> Somebody **has been sleeping** in my bed! The bed sheets are still rumpled.

> Somebody **has slept** in my bed. This could have happened yesterday.

With some verbs (*live*, *work*, *teach*) both the present perfect and the present perfect progressive have essentially the same meaning.

> I have lived here since 1994 = I **have been living** here since 1994.

EXERCISE 11

Now write questions with *How long*. Use the present perfect or the present perfect progressive.

Example:

Right now Nanda is practicing his trumpet playing.

How Long

has he been practicing?

1. His mother hates horn music.

2. His mother is thinking of buying earplugs.

3. Nanda has a big problem.

4. Nanda is tone deaf.

5. His mother is looking for another instrument for her son.

6. Nanda wants a guitar.

CLASS EXERCISE

Write the answer in the space provided.

1. Pierre has changed a tire.

Aziz has been changing a tire.

Whose clothes are more likely to be dirty?

2. Mr. White has been drinking strong coffee.

Mr. Green has drunk strong coffee.

Who feels jittery now? _____

3. Marnie has yelled for twenty minutes.

Natalia has been yelling for twenty minutes.

Whose vocal cords are getting sore? _____

4. Mary has lived in Nova Scotia for years.

Claire has been living in Nova Scotia for years.

Is there any difference between these sentences? _____

EXERCISE 12

Use the present perfect or the present perfect progressive. In some cases, either tense may be used.

1. Mutt: Where is the subway?

Jeff: The subway isn't far from here. I (walk) _____
there many times.

Mutt: I'm getting tired. We (walk) _____ for six hours.
You said that the subway wasn't far!

Jeff: You're just out of shape. Well, here we are. Hey, Joe, how long (you, wait)
_____ for the subway train?

Joe: I (wait) _____ for about 10 minutes.

2. I'm going crazy. That baby (cry) _____ for two hours. I
(see, never) _____ a baby that cries so much.

3. My hand is getting sore. I (write) _____ for two hours. I
(write) _____ over one hundred invitations.

4. The Berezans (live) _____ on my street since 1976.

5. Jim: (be, you) _____ able to reach your sister on the
phone yet?

Bob: Not yet. I (try) _____ for the last 15 minutes.

The Past Perfect Tenses

The past perfect is formed with *had* and the past participle. For example: *Yesterday we went to see* Evita *even though we had seen it twice.*

As long as a story about a past event contains a very sequential order, you can probably stick to regular past tenses. However, sometimes you need to reach further back into the more distant past in order to explain something. For example:

> When we were children, Jack and I went for a walk in the fields near my farm. As we were passing a large rock, we heard a rattle. Beside the rock a rattlesnake was coiled up and ready to strike. Jack screamed with shock because he had never seen a snake before, but I remained calm, and we slowly backed up to get away from the snake. Afterwards, I teased Jack and mimicked his frightened reaction.

Jack's lack of experience with snakes predates the events in the story. Therefore, when you tell a story about a past event, you can use the past perfect to go back to an earlier past time.

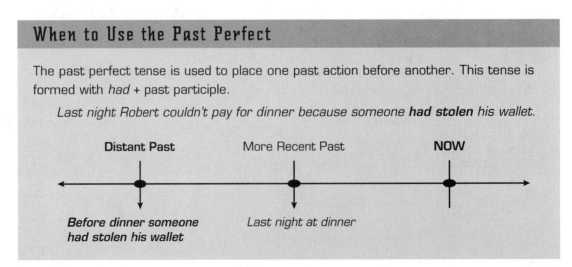

When to Use the Past Perfect

The past perfect tense is used to place one past action before another. This tense is formed with *had* + past participle.

*Last night Robert couldn't pay for dinner because someone **had stolen** his wallet.*

Distant Past	More Recent Past	NOW

Before dinner someone had stolen his wallet

Last night at dinner

CLASS EXERCISE

Do you understand the difference between the simple past and the past perfect? Answer the following questions and explain your answers.

1. When Sonia got to the 1996 Olympics in Atlanta, she had won a silver medal.

    When Margaret got to the 1996 Olympics in Atlanta, she won a silver medal.

    Who was already an Olympic champion when she got to the 1996 Olympics?

    _____

    _____

    _____

2. When Andrew arrived at the theater, the music had started.

    When Marcel arrived at the theater, the music started.

    Who missed part of the show?

    _____

    _____

    _____

3. At 8 o'clock this morning, Monica had her coffee.

    At 8 o'clock this morning, Susan had had her coffee.

    Who was drinking her coffee at 8 o'clock?

    _____

    _____

    _____

4. When the second robbery occurred, Frank had just been arrested.

    When the second robbery occurred, Phillip was arrested.

    Who could not have committed the second robbery?

    _____

    _____

    _____

5. Beth had the chicken pox when Pedro visited her.

    Helen had had the chicken pox when Pedro visited her.

    Who was sick in bed when Pedro visited?

    _____

    _____

    _____

EXERCISE 1

Fill in the blanks with the simple past or the past perfect.

1. My sister (watch) _____ *Pulp Fiction* with me last night

even though she (see, already) _____ it twice.

2. When I (call) _____ Jennifer, her father (say)

_____ that she (move) _____

to Ottawa. I (just, want) _____ to know if Jennifer

had the novel *The Catcher in the Rye* that she (borrow)

_____ from me.

3. When we (arrive) _____ at the restaurant, our friends

(be) _____ no longer there. They (leave, already)

_____ . Later that night, we (call)

_____ them to apologize and also to find out why

they (wait, not) _____ for us.

4. Last Easter, my wife and I (cancel) _____ our flight to

Florida because the pilots (go) _____ on strike a week

earlier.

EXERCISE 2

Circle the correct verb tense to complete the sentences in the following paragraphs.

Yesterday my friend Tim (1. *quit* / *had quit*) his job. Many people thought that
Tim (2. *quit* / *had quit*) his job months ago. Tim loved his job, but to my knowledge
Tim (3. *made* / *had made*) several errors in the months before he left the job.

I'm sure that when Tim (4. *left* / *had left*) the office yesterday it (5. *was* / *had
been*) a very emotional moment for him. Last night I talked to Tim's wife about it.
When Tim (6. *arrived* / *had arrived*) home yesterday, he explained to his wife what he
(7. *did* / *had done*) and she (8. *told* / *had told*) him that she (9. *understood* / *had
understood*) completely.

CLASS EXERCISE

Fill in the blanks with the simple past or the past perfect tense.

1. Once upon a time there lived a man named Arthur, son of the king. Arthur (know, not) _____ that he was really the king's child because, in his entire life, he (live, never) _____ with the king. One day, quite by chance, Arthur (take) _____ part in a tournament to choose the next king. There was a contest: whoever could pull the magic sword, Excalibur, out of the stone would be declared the next king. Arthur (pull) _____ the sword out of the stone; therefore, Arthur (become) _____ king. Right after becoming king, Arthur (marry) _____ a beautiful woman named Guinevere, and later he (go) _____ off to war.

2. After the long war, Arthur (return) _____ home and (discover) _____ that his wife (become) _____ friends with a knight called Lancelot. Things started to go terribly wrong when Arthur (come) _____ upon Lancelot and Guinevere sleeping naked in the grass. Arthur left his sword next to them on the ground, to show the adulterous couple that he (see) _____ them, and then he left the scene. When Lancelot (awake) _____ from his lover's embrace, he realized, upon seeing the sword, that Arthur (be) _____ there. Lancelot immediately (run) _____ away.

Past Perfect Progressive

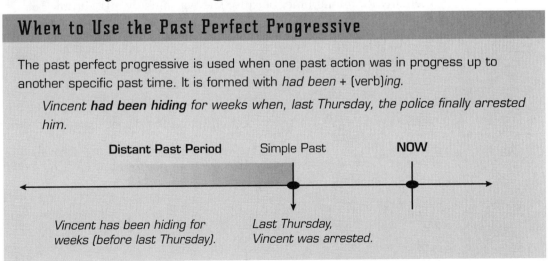

When to Use the Past Perfect Progressive

The past perfect progressive is used when one past action was in progress up to another specific past time. It is formed with *had been* + (verb)*ing*.

*Vincent **had been hiding** for weeks when, last Thursday, the police finally arrested him.*

| | Distant Past Period | Simple Past | NOW |

Vincent has been hiding for weeks (before last Thursday).

Last Thursday, Vincent was arrested.

EXERCISE 3

Fill in the spaces with either the past perfect or the past perfect progressive.

1. Yesterday evening I was very tired because I (exercise) _____ for hours.

2. When the seven dwarfs returned home, they realized that someone (live) _____ in their home. They found a girl called Snow White in Grumpy's bed. She (sleep) _____ in his bed for several hours.

3. Last night my father put the cat out at 8 p.m. because the cat (be, not) _____ out all day. Not much later he opened the door and let the cat in because our crazy cat (meow) _____ for twenty minutes.

EXERCISE 4

Complete the exercise using any simple or progressive tense.

1. Last Friday, when I (arrive) _____ at the party, Alexia (wait) _____ for me. She (wait) _____ for two hours and she (be) _____ a little upset. When she saw me, she (run) _____ up to me and she told me that she (spend) _____ the evening all alone, because she (know, not) _____ anybody in the room.

2. I explained to her that I (lose) _____ the paper with the address of the party on it. I think that Alexia (wait) _____ at the party for a long time, because she was already a bit drunk.

Past Perfect Tenses in the Passive Voice

The passive form of the past perfect is formed with *had been* + the past participle.

Active: *Last night there was nothing left on the dinner table. My brother **had eaten** the food.*

Passive: *Last night there was nothing left on the dinner table. The food **had been eaten** by my brothers.*

5 The Future Tenses

The future tenses are relatively simple to use for intermediate-level students. When you use *will*, there are no verbs to conjugate, and no irregular verb lists to memorize. For example: *Next year I will move, my sister will stay here, my brother will buy a house, and we will remain close.* Notice that no *s* is necessary on third person singular verbs.

The future *be going to* form sometimes confuses students. Often students write *gonna* because that is what they hear English people saying. However, *gonna* is not a word and should not be written. Always use the form *is, am* or *are going to*.

Most of the time you can use both *will* and *be going to* to predict a future action, but, as is explained below, there are instances where either one or the other must be used.

Pay particular attention to the section entitled *Future Tenses: Time Clauses*, because there are cases where the future tense form cannot be used in English, even if it is used in other languages in the same situation.

Future

Will *vs.* Be Going To

Although both *will* and *be going to* can be used to make predictions about the future, there are some instances where you must use either one or the other.

Use *will* when you decide to do something at the time of speaking. You are "willing" to do it.

> *The phone is ringing. I **will** answer it.*

Use *be going to* when you have planned to do something before you talk about it.

> *I'm **going to** visit Ottawa next week. I have my train ticket.*

EXERCISE 1

Put the verb into the correct form, using *will* or *be going to*. In some cases, either one may be used.

1. I feel sick so I (visit) _____ the doctor.

2. The phone is ringing. I (get) _____ it.

3. Dorothy is pregnant. She (have) _____ a girl.

4. I have a lot of work to do so I (stay) _____ home tomorrow.

5. That's the doorbell. I (get) _____ it.

6. On my next vacation, I (visit) _____ Halifax. I have already bought the ticket.

7. I (make) _____ the coffee if you're too busy.

8. According to the radio broadcast, it (snow) _____ tonight.

9. Mike (do) _____ the dishes if you're too busy.

10. In the future I (be) _____ a lawyer or a notary.

Future Tenses: Time Clauses

In future sentences, use the present tense verb form after time markers.

*I'll **call** you when I **get** home.*

*She **will meet** you as soon as she **finishes** work.*

*We **won't eat** supper until Anne **arrives**.*

The rule applies for all verbs that follow these time markers:

when	before	as soon as	as long as
after	unless	until	in case
if			while

EXERCISE 2

Complete the following future tense sentences with the verbs in parentheses.

Example: Mary (come) *will come* if you (ask) *ask* her.

1. I (call) _____ you as soon as I (arrive) _____ in Paris next week.

2. When Monica (quit) _____ her job next Friday, everyone (be) _____ very happy.

3. I (eat) _____ the rest of the cake if you (finish)

_____ the cookies.

4. Hugh (talk) _____ to Ron about it as soon as Ron (get)

_____ here.

5. Anne (do) _____ the work alone unless she really (need)

_____ us.

6. When I (have) _____ some spare time, I (help)

_____ Toby with his math homework.

7. We (take care) _____ of the dog until the vet (arrive)

_____ .

8. I (go, not) _____ unless you (go) _____ too.

9. As soon as the weather (get) _____ colder, Beth (go)

_____ skiing with us.

10. We (prepare) _____ the meal tomorrow in case we (have,

not) _____ time on the weekend.

Future Tenses in the Passive Voice

To form the passive voice in the future tense, simply write *will be* or *are going to be* +
the past participle.

Active	Passive
Pierre **will do** the dishes later.	*The dishes **will be done** later [by Pierre].*
Alex is going to dry the dishes.	*The dishes **are going to be dried** [by Alex].*

EXERCISE 3

Change the following active sentences into the passive form. Use the appropriate verb
tense.

Example: Jo is going to build our kitchen cabinets.

The kitchen cabinets are going to be built by Jo.

1. Someone will deliver the order.

_____

2. Jo's company, Woodwork, builds sturdy furniture.

_____

3. Last year Jo built a desk.

_____

4. The company will hire ten new people next year.

_____

5. Those new employees are going to need homes.

_____

Now change the following passive sentences to the active form.

   Example: A new hockey arena is needed (by the town).

   The town needs a new hockey arena.

6. Part-time jobs have been created by the government.

_____

7. Money is needed for the new hockey team.

_____

8. Money has been donated by the public.

_____

9. The project is going to be financed by the recreation committee.

_____

10. Parents will be invited to the opening of the new arena (by the organizers).

_____

CLASS EXERCISE

Part 1: Fill in the blanks with the present or future tense.

1. I've heard that banks are planning to replace all bank tellers with bank machines in the future. If the banks (replace) _____ tellers with machines, there (be) _____ disastrous consequences for the economy. When the tellers (have, not) _____ jobs anymore, they (need) _____ to receive government assistance, and every worker in Canada will have to pay for that.

2. Some banks claim that all tellers (retrain) _____ by the banks, and that very few people (lose) _____ their jobs, but I find that very hard to believe. When four or five people (run) _____ a bank branch instead of fifteen or twenty, then obviously many people (lay off) _____ by the banks!

Part 2: Proofread and correct any future tense errors.

3. The average consumer will also suffer if machines will replace humans. As soon as a person will need advice, or as soon as a customer will have a problem, it will take a machine longer to solve the problem.

4. A lot of people dislike dealing with a machine. The world will be a very impersonal place when all of our daily transactions will be done with a machine.

Embedded Questions

When a question is part of a larger sentence (embedded), no longer use the special question word order. An auxiliary after the question word is not needed.

Question   Embedded Question

    Auxiliary

What *do* you want for lunch?   He wonders *what you want for lunch.*

Use *if* or *whether* if there is no question word.

   Auxiliary

   Did you finish your salad?   He wonders *if you finished your salad.*

   Will you help me, please?   I want to know *whether you will help me.*

EXERCISE 4

Make a new sentence from these questions.

    Example: What does "itch" mean?

                I wonder *what "itch" means.*

1. What is Dan doing?

She wants to know _____

2. Where does Dan live?

She wonders _____

3. Why are the guests late?

I would like to know _____

4. How long will the party last?

He wonders _____

5. Does Gina smoke?

Can you tell me _____

6. What is that police officer doing?

She wonders _____

7. How long has he been there?

Do you know _____

8. What time did she leave?

Can you tell me _____

9. When will we leave?

I wonder _____

10. Is Kim going to watch the parade?

I would like to know _____

Present Tenses with a Future Meaning

You can use the present progressive tense to talk about a previously planned event.

*This week, my son **is playing hockey** on Monday, and he **is going to** the dentist on Wednesday.*

You can use the simple present when you talk about schedules and timetables.

*What time **does** the show **begin**?*

*The train **leaves** at midnight.*

*The football game **starts** at 2 p.m. tomorrow.*

EXERCISE 5

Complete the conversation with the words in parentheses. Use the present progressive or the simple present to indicate the future.

1. Kali: What (you, do) _____ this evening?

2. Sandra: Andrew and I (go) _____ to a play. Can you come

with us?

3. Kali: I can't. I (take) _____ my little sister shopping.

4. Sandra: Well, the play (start) _____ at 7:30 p.m. Before the

play we (plan) _____ to go to a coffee shop. Maybe

we could all meet for coffee downtown.

5. Kali: How (you, go) _____ downtown? You (drive, not)

_____ , are you? It's impossible to park downtown!

6. Sandra: No, we (drive, not) _____ . We (take)

_____ the bus. It (leave) _____

every half hour.

Future Progressive vs. Future Perfect

These two future tenses can be tricky. Study the two boxes below, and see if you can make the distinction between the future progressive and the future perfect in the exercises that follow.

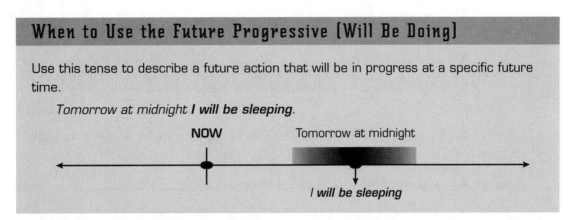

When to Use the Future Progressive (Will Be Doing)

Use this tense to describe a future action that will be in progress at a specific future time.

*Tomorrow at midnight **I will be sleeping.***

NOW — Tomorrow at midnight — *I will be sleeping*

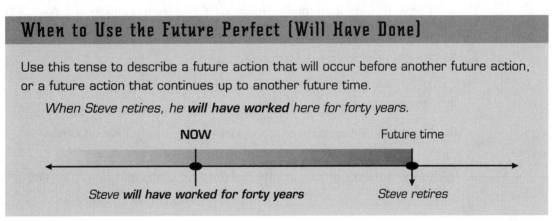

When to Use the Future Perfect (Will Have Done)

Use this tense to describe a future action that will occur before another future action, or a future action that continues up to another future time.

*When Steve retires, he **will have worked** here for forty years.*

NOW — Future time — Steve **will have worked for forty years** — *Steve retires*

CLASS EXERCISE

Answer the following questions.

1. Joe will be cooking supper when his wife arrives home from work.

Sam will have cooked supper when his wife arrives home from work.

Whose wife will eat first? _____

2. Next Saturday, Nadine will be finishing her work.

Next Saturday, Sandra will have finished her work.

Who gets to spend next Saturday relaxing? _____

3. Tonight at mealtime, Michael will have studied.

Tonight at mealtime, Diego will be studying.

Who will have his books at the supper table? _____

EXERCISE 6

Make sentences with the future perfect (will have done) or the future progressive (will be doing).

1. When I retire in the year 2020, I (work) _____ for 40 years.

2. On Sunday Gary plays chess from noon to 5 p.m., so on Sunday at 3:30 p.m. he (play) _____ chess.

3. Next month I (live) _____ with Gary for exactly 10 years.

4. I have only three dollars left in my bank account. If I'm not careful, I (spend) _____ all my money before my next paycheck comes!

5. Don't plan to watch the news at my place tonight. By 10 p.m. I (go) _____ to bed.

6. When I retire, in 25 years, I (work) _____ for more than half my life.

7. I have to work late this evening, so if you try to call me at 7 p.m., I (work) _____ .

8. By the time we finish the project, it (take) _____ over three years to complete.

9. What (you, do) _____ tomorrow at noon?

10. Tomorrow when I arrive at the station, my mother's train (arrive) _____ and she (wait) _____ for me in the station's restaurant. By the time we get home from the station, Mom (tell) _____ me all of the family gossip.

CLASS EXERCISE

Find and correct the errors, if necessary.

1. She will help us finish the job unless she will be too tired.

2. By tomorrow, Angie has been in Canada for exactly four years.

3. I will apply for a job when I will finish my schooling.

4. I go to bed at 10 p.m. Tonight at midnight I will sleep.

5. When I will get home later, I will phone my mother.

6. By the year 2010, she will be a scientist for 30 years.

7. In case you will not have any spare time, I will mow the lawn.

8. The phone is ringing. I am going to answer it!

9. I will listen to the radio while you are going to fix the television.

10. We won't eat dinner until Allison will arrive.

Review of Chapters 1 to 5

CLASS EXERCISE A: PRESENT TENSES REVIEW

Fill in the blanks with the simple present or the present progressive tense. (20 points)

1. Judy: What (happen) _____ with you these days?

2. Maya: Not much. Look over there! What (that girl, try) _____ to do?

3. Judy: I (think) _____ that she is in trouble. What (she, say) _____ to that man over there?

4. Maya: I (know, not) _____ . Maybe she (tell) _____ him to get lost.

5. Judy: Oh look. The man (leave) _____ . He (seem) _____ to be in a hurry. (you, suppose) _____ he is dangerous?

6. Maya: Well, he (appear) _____ to be a little eccentric. He (wear) _____ orange cowboy boots, and he (have) _____ a feather in his cap. Now the girl (walk) _____ towards us. (you, know) _____ her?

7. Judy: No. Maybe she (know) _____ that we (discuss) _____ her. What (you, think) _____ she (want) _____ with us?

8. Maya: Maybe she simply (want) _____ to know why we (stare) _____ at her.

CLASS EXERCISE B: SUBJECT-VERB AGREEMENT

Add *s* to all third-person singular verbs. The verb *be* has already been conjugated. There are 14 verbs to conjugate.

(1) A study have been made by a primatologist who look at the way that gorillas interact. The study focus on a group of gorillas from a central African nation. A group from the U.S.A. regularly send money for the study and supply the female primatologist, Ms. Windlow, with equipment and staff. Her equipment include tents, a computer, a fax machine and cooking equipment. Ms. Windlow hire local people to help find and examine the gorillas. The research grant contain extra money so that the primatologist can go home twice a year.

(2) The research focus on one particular group of gorillas. The study examine the social hierarchy in that gorilla group, and explain how one young female gorilla take care of her babies. Although there is sporadic fighting in the region, the primatologist insist that she is completely safe, and she absolutely refuse to leave the area.

CLASS EXERCISE C: PAST TENSES REVIEW

Underline and correct the past tense errors in the following sentences.

1. Jamie didn't wanted to go to the show yesterday.

2. The two best things about my previous job was that I could get free hockey tickets, and that I had Fridays off.

3. While Bill frying something on the stove, the fire alarm went off. We call the alarm our "burnt-food detector."

4. Why didn't he stay at the farm with us last night? Didn't you asked him to join us?

5. Yesterday, we were receiving a very disturbing letter from our bank.

6. The young couple didn't noticed that their car was being towed away.

7. At last night's party, when the police arrived, 40 people danced in the room.

8. Although I rarely read novels, last week I choosed to read Winston Groom's novel, *Forrest Gump*.

9. Where you found the Winston Groom novel? Was it in the library?

10. There was several copies of the novel in the main branch of the library.

CLASS EXERCISE D: PRESENT, PAST, AND PRESENT PERFECT REVIEW

Write the verbs in the correct tense in the space provided.

Dear Shyamal,

Thank you for your letter. I realize that I (write, not) _____ to you for many years. I (have, not) _____ an excuse for that, other than to say that in recent years my life (become) _____ increasingly busy. I (have) _____ a full-time job and two children, but I know that I really have no excuse for not writing.

I imagine that your life (change) _____ a lot since our last meeting. How (everybody, do) _____ over there? I (be, not) _____ back to Asia since that first voyage twelve years ago.

India (undergo) _____ many changes since my visit there. When I (visit) _____ you in 1984, almost nobody had televisions. At that time, the Indian government (allow, not) _____ foreign-made electrical goods into India. During my year in India, I once (meet) _____ an American girl on a bus who, at that moment, (smuggle) _____ a Japanese-made VCR into India. The laws (change) _____ in recent years, and now foreign goods can be imported into India.

(you, be) _____ to Shantiniketan recently? That was one of the most beautiful places that I (ever, see) _____ . In fact, I (be, never) _____ to a village or town since then that could compare.

CLASS EXERCISE E: QUESTIONS PRACTICE

Write the questions for the following answers. The specific answer is in bold.

1. Willy has been a carpenter **for twelve years**.

_____

2. Nadine bought **some used books** when she was in Boston.

_____

3. Elsa asked **Richard** to go to the party with her.

_____

4. The baby has been sleeping **for four hours**.

_____

5. Vincent does the dishes **every morning at 6 a.m.**

_____

6. Trish and Elise have been to **20 countries**.

_____

7. Last winter, we stayed in Mexico City **for two months**.

_____

8. **Alicia** gave me that leather handbag yesterday.

_____

9. The museum is about **four kilometers** from Alicia's home.

_____

10. Karen goes to her doctor **every six months**.

_____

CLASS EXERCISE F: ALL TENSE REVIEW

Highlight the tense that is most appropriate. (20 answers)

1. Right now Fred (*is preparing / prepare / prepares*) dinner. Tim isn't helping because he (*has / have / is having*) a cold.

2. The phone is ringing again. I (*am going to answer / will answer*) it, unless you (*think / will think*) it is for you.

3. In 1992, when Dominique started working at the advertising agency, she (*never used / has never used / had never used*) a computer before. Now she is very good on the computer because she (*use / is using / uses*) one every day.

4. While William (*washing / was washing / washed*) the dishes last night, I (*hear / heard / was hearing*) a loud crash. I (*run / ran / have run / had run*) into the kitchen and almost cried because he (*had dropped / has dropped / dropped*) our brand new crystal bowl.

5. When I bumped into my childhood friend on the street last week, we (*don't recognized / didn't recognize / hadn't recognized*) each other immediately. When he began to talk to me, I realized that I (*saw / have seen / had seen*) him before because I (*recognized / have recognized / had recognized*) his voice. Next Tuesday, we (*meet / are going to meet / will meet*) for coffee at Murray's Café, unless something unexpected (*will come / is going to come / come / comes*) up.

6. Marco always (*act / acts / is acting*) very inconsistently. Some days, when I (*passed / pass / passes*) him in the hall, he (*smile / smiles / is smiling*), and says "hello." But on other days, he is downright rude. Tomorrow, when I (*will see / see / sees*) him, he probably (*doesn't greet / won't greets / won't greet*) me.

CLASS EXERCISE G: ALL TENSES REVIEW (INCLUDING PASSIVE VOICE)

Fill in the blanks with the appropriate tense. The verb may be in the active or the passive voice. (15 answers)

1. When she was a teenager Carolyn and her boyfriend (involve)

_____ in several crimes. Although Carolyn (never, arrest)

_____ during her teen years, her boyfriend Carl (arrest)

_____ several times since 1985. Now Carol has her act

together, and last year she (hire) _____ at a graphic

design company. She (see, not) _____ Carl since 1992,

even though he (try) _____ on several occasions to

contact her.

2. Traditionally, soldiers who (conscript) _____ are

youthful. My great uncle was only eighteen when he (go)

_____ to fight in World War II. When he was sent

overseas, (never, see) _____ death, and he (traumatize)

_____ by what he saw in Europe. He is now a very old

man, and he rarely (discuss) _____ the war years.

3. More individuals in our society will lose hope if we (neglect)

_____ to address the unemployment issue. A great

number of companies (downsize) _____ since the

1980's, and this is contributing to the high unemployment rate.

4. Since the 1970's, disaster films (be) _____ very popular.

Almost every natural catastrophe (explore) _____ by

American filmmakers, including floods, tornadoes, and fires.

Tense Review Chart

May 5, 1994	TODAY	Year 2020

Future
will / going to

Present Perfect
Past time(s) unknown
?

Present Perfect
Past time continues to present

Present Progressive
Action is in progress now

Future Perfect
Action continues
up to a future
time (2020)

Past Progressive
Action was in progress
on past date

Simple Past
Past time is known

Past Perfect
Distant past before
another past

Simple Present—Action is a fact or habit

CLASS EXERCISE H: ALL TENSES REVIEW

Using the verb chart to help you, name the tense used in each of the following sentences.
Then, *in the space provided, briefly state why that tense was used.*

		Verb Tense	Why Tense was Used
		Simple present	*Action is a fact*
1.	Humans **need** food and water to survive.		
2.	My day usually **begins** with a cup of coffee, and toast.		
3.	I **am presently working** as a fashion designer.		
4.	I **started** my job on May 5, 1994.		
5.	On that day in 1994, I **was walking** past this building when I saw a sign in the window.		
6.	I **had never worked** as a designer before then.		
7.	I **have been** at this company since 1994.		
8.	My boss and I **have gone** to Paris several times on business trips.		
9.	I **will probably quit** my job in the year 2020.		
10.	By the time that I quit, I **will have worked** for most of my life in the fashion industry.		

6 Problems with Plurals

Students may feel comfortable with their use of regular and irregular plural nouns. However, there are some problems that even advanced students sometimes have with plurals. For example, in both Spanish and French, adjectives take a plural form. But *las cosas bonitas* and *les belles choses* become *beautiful things* in English, because English adjectives don't have plural forms.

This section contains four rules, given in the "Plural Tip" boxes.

Irregular Plurals

Plural Tip 1

Irregular plurals do not need an additional *s*.

EXERCISE 1

Write the plural form of the following nouns in the spaces provided.

1. man _____
2. goose _____
3. child _____
4. woman _____
5. gentleman _____
6. person _____

One Of The ... *and* Each/Every

EXERCISE 2

Each sentence has one plural error. Circle the error, and write the correct word in the space provided.

1. You must study each grammar rules very carefully. _____

2. Those parents think that their children's want too many Christmas presents. _____

3. Although it is disturbing for us, many directors like to make violent film. _____

4. Every Christmas the childrens make their parents take them to see Santa Claus. _____

5. One of the best director in the world will be at the Montreal Film Festival. _____

6. There is a big difference between men who like women and the one who don't. _____

7. I will show you some example of how people write incorrectly. _____

8. There are a lot of show on TV that are very bad. _____

9. One of the most interesting special that I've ever seen was on PBS TV. _____

10. Criminals often have many reason for their evil actions. _____

11. The people who live in those small houses take good care of each others. _____

12. Every characters in that TV show is really funny. _____

Non-count Nouns

Plural Tip 3

Non-count nouns do not take a plural form.

If you can't put a number directly before a noun (a person, place or thing), then it cannot be counted.

Look at the differences in these sentences:

1. Those tables are very expensive. I'm going to buy two tables.
2. That furniture is very expensive. I'm going to buy some furniture.

In the first sentence, *tables* can be counted. It takes an *s*. In the second sentence, *furniture* cannot be counted, so it cannot take an *s*. If you want to count a non-count noun, you must begin with an expression like "one piece of," "twenty pieces of."

Some Non-count Nouns

Non-count nouns include "category" names (such as *mail*) which cannot be counted. *Types* of mail can be counted, however (letter, package, etc. .)

luggage	news	equipment
jewelry	furniture	music
homework	machinery	money

Non-count nouns also include abstract nouns, such as the following:

advice	education	evidence
information	health	help
knowledge	violence	research

With non-count nouns, use *much* and *a little*.

How **much homework** do you have?   I just have a **little homework** tonight.

With count nouns use *many* and *a few*.

How **many suitcases** do you have?   I just have a **few bags**.

EXERCISE 3

Write *much* or *many* in the spaces provided.

1. How _____ money do you have in your wallet?

2. How _____ electricity do you need to power that stove?

3. Carl is a loner. He doesn't have _____ friends.

4. The dog is shedding its hair. It doesn't have _____ hair left.

5. There isn't _____ information that I can give you. Call back later.

6. How _____ luggage do you have? Do you have _____ suitcases?

7. There are _____ houses in that new development. Unfortunately, there are too _____ acts of violence in that town.

8. I thought you said that there isn't _____ violence around this area?

9. How _____ pages of homework do you have tonight?

10. My late grandfather didn't have _____ different jobs in his life. Because there wasn't _____ work available, he remained a farmer throughout his life.

Write *a few* or *a little* in the spaces provided.

11. We need _____ more hangers in this closet.

12. Could you give me _____ help? I can't start my car.

13. Pilo knows _____ French grammar. He knows _____ words in English.

14. Can you lend me _____ more money? I need _____ more dollars.

15. I can meet you for _____ minutes. I have _____ free time now.

Adjectives

Plural Tip 4

Adjectives (which describe nouns) do not take a plural form.

   Incorrect: *Those are the problems students.*
   Correct: *Those are the **problem** students.*

Be aware that adjectives may appear after the verb *be*.

   Those cars are **expensive**.

   Your ideas are **very interesting**.

CLASS EXERCISE

Try using these adjectives in a short descriptive paragraph. You could describe a close friend or family member.

Some Adjectives

Personality Traits		Physical Appearance		Physical Traits
sensitive	selfish	striking	tall	whiskery
sensible	proud	handsome	slender	wrinkled
gentle	nervous	homely	plump	dimpled
kind	flighty	overweight	heavy set	balding
rude	obnoxious	skinny	muscular	curly (hair)
stingy	witty	pale	athletic	
sympathetic	easygoing	gorgeous		hazel (eyes)
friendly	shy			cleft (chin)

EXERCISE 4

There are errors in these sentences of the following types: incorrect plural form or the incorrect use of *much* or *many*. If the sentence is correct, write *C* in the space provided. If the sentence has an error, correct it in the space provided.

1. There are many unexplained naturals events.   *natural events*

2. It's possible that one day there will be no more whale.

3. Santa brings hope to every childrens in the world.

4. Teenagers are causing too much accidents.

5. It's important for many children to be at the party.

6. In *Dumb and Dumber*, Harry and Lloyd dream of being earth worms breeders.

7. There are a lot of TV shows that are really stupids.

8. I carefully watched each moments of the play.

9. Salinger is one of the best writer of this century.

10. We search for some simples explanations about the meaning of life.

11. Her questions are always very intelligents.

12. She doesn't have much informations to give you. _____

13. Gerry has many funny pieces of advice to give you. _____

14. There isn't many violence in these streets. _____

15. That is one of the worst show on television. _____

CLASS EXERCISE: PLURAL FORM

Add *s* to any noun that requires a plural form, or rewrite the noun in its irregular plural form. There are 15 nouns that must be changed from the singular to the plural form.

"Many *child* have no food" would be changed to "Many *children* have no food."

(1) At the present time, there are very few job available. Many person have decided to create their own job. Here are some simple piece of advice that could help you to plan your own business.

(2) First, you have to think of something that isn't already being done extensively. If you want to break into an existing market, it's a good idea to create new contact, and to verify if one of your competitor is already in the region.

(3) If possible, try to develop a product that doesn't already exist. Original idea, like the one by the creator of the hula hoop, can seem simple, yet this idea eventually turned the inventor into a millionaire. Although you can't expect to earn two million dollar immediately, you can expect to turn a profit in the long term. An accountant once told me that every new business should have a four-year plan. In other word, it could take four year before the business hits the break-even point.

(4) Many people always forget an important step. They forget to ask knowledgeable individual for information and piece of advice. We can't all be good in every field, and we must recognize our weakness and be prepared to ask for help.

(5) If you lack information in a particular area, you could take extra course in your free time. You don't have to hurry. You may need to take several year to plan your business. It can take a lot of time to complete a project successfully.

Modals

Modals (or modal auxiliary verbs, as they are also known) are used when we say that events are possible or probable, or when we want to refer to willingness, ability, obligation or advice.

Don't add *s* to modals or to the verbs that follow them, because modals have no *s* form for the third person singular. For example: *I should work late and Sharon must stay here. The boss could let us leave but he wouldn't do that.* Notice that none of the auxiliaries or verbs have an *s*.

The idiom *have to* has been added to the following list of modals, mainly because it has the same meaning as another modal, and means *necessity*. However, *have to* is not, strictly speaking, a modal, and it does have a third person singular form, *has to*, which is used with *he*, *she* and *it*. Unlike other modals, *have to* requires the auxiliary *do* or *does* in the question and negative forms.

Just as modals don't change to take an *s*, the actual modal also doesn't change when you talk about a past time. You either use another modal (for example, *I can speak German* becomes *I could speak German* in the past time) or you add *have* and the past participle to the modal to indicate a past time (for example, *She should sleep* becomes *She should have slept* in the past time).

The modal *shall* has not been included on the list mainly because it is rarely used in North America. However, if you are interested, *shall* could be used in place of *should* when asking a polite question. *Shall I help you? Shall* can also be used instead of *will* to indicate a future action (for example, *I shall phone you tomorrow*).

Using Modals

Modals in Present and Past Tenses

Summary of Modals in Present and Past Tenses

Modal Form	Usage	Present Tense	Past Tense
Can	*ability*	She **can** speak German.	could speak
Could	a) *possibility* b) *polite request*	Alice **could** lend you $10. **Could** I borrow a $20?	could have lent
Should	a) *giving advice* b) *expectation*	You **should** see a doctor. The storm **should** hit soon.	should have seen
Ought to	*same meaning as "should"*	You **ought** to see a doctor.	ought to have seen
May	a) *possibility* b) *polite request*	It **may** be a mouse. **May** I help you?	may have been
Might	*possibility*	I **might** go to a movie.	might have gone
Must	a) *necessity* b) *probability*	You **must** do your work. She **must** be ill.	had to do must have been
Would	a) *conditional* b) *preference* c) *polite request*	She **would** call if . . . I **would rather** have a tea. **Would** you like a cup of tea?	would have called
Have to	*necessity*	She **has to** work late.	had to work

ORAL ACTIVITY

Answer the following questions.

1. Which two have the same meaning?
   a. John ought to pay for the sitter.
   b. John could pay for the sitter.
   c. John should pay for the sitter.

2. Which sentence is most polite? Least polite?
   a. May I use your phone?
   b. Can I borrow your phone?
   c. Could I borrow your phone?

3. Which two have the same meaning?
   a. That bank might close this year.
   b. That bank must close this year.
   c. That bank may close this year.

4. Which employee had no choice?
   a. Jose had to run home.
   b. Martin must have run home.
   c. Anne had better run home.

5. Which speaker is most certain?
   a. Nadia: That black spot must be ink.
   b. Rosy: That black spot has to be ink.
   c. Aline: That black spot may be ink.

6. Which person has a choice?
   a. The doctor must work overtime.
   b. The nurse may stay late tonight.
   c. The orderly has to work all night.

Modals: Question Form

All modals (except *have to*) act as auxiliaries. To form a question, move the modal before the subject.

Statement	Question form
I (can) hear you.	(Can) you hear me?
She should eat those carrots.	**Should** she eat those carrots?
Henry has to work late.	**Does** Henry **have to** work late?

EXERCISE 1

Make questions for the following answers. The specific answer to the question is in bold.

1. **Yes**, Diego should go to the hospital.

_____

2. He has to go there **tomorrow**.

_____

3. **No**, he can't eat or drink after midnight.

_____

4. Well, he should bring **slippers** with him.

_____

5. **Yes**, he has to go into the operating room without his parents.

_____

6. His parents must wait **outside** the operating room during the operation.

_____

7. **Yes**, they can go into the recovery room with him.

_____

Modals: Negative Forms

Examine the negative forms of the following modals. Notice that *have to* needs an auxiliary.

Statement	Negative	Negative contraction
He should work harder.	He **should not** work harder.	*shouldn't*
He could have stayed home.	He **could not have stayed** home.	*couldn't have stayed*
Brian has to do it.	Brian **does** not **have to** do it.	*doesn't have to*

EXERCISE 2

Make the modals in the following sentences negative.

Example: Eric should call me.   *should not call* (or *shouldn't*)

1. Melanie has to exercise more often.   _____

2. Ellen can help him.   _____

3. Rebecca would like a coffee.   _____

4. Helen had to phone home right away.   _____

5. The cat could be at the neighbor's house.   _____

6. Isaac should have done his homework yesterday. _____

7. She could have done more work.   _____

8. He must have seen the accident.   _____

CLASS EXERCISE

Does *must* indicate (*P*) Probability or (*N*) Necessity in the following sentences?

Example: Someone is at the door. It must be Simon.   *P*

1. Carol isn't home. She must still be at school.   _____

2. He must run to the toilet because he feels ill.   _____

3. That light must be a UFO. There is no other explanation. _____

4. Those lizards must live in a warm environment or they will die. _____

5. The spots on your sleeve must have been ketchup from your hot dog. _____

EXERCISE 3

Change the sentences to the past tense. Remember to use the appropriate past form of *must*.

Must meaning *Necessity*: past form is *had to*
Must meaning *Probability*: past form is *must have* + past participle

Example: Monica *has to help* the patients.   *had to help*

1. Her brother *must be* in an accident.   _____

2. Her brother, Terry, *has to get* stitches.   _____

3. Kevin *should clean* his hair thoroughly.   _____

4. Kevin *must have* lice.   _____

5. Pepino *could help* us.   _____

6. Arnold *must work* overtime. (He has no choice.) _____

7. The doctors *should be* more careful.   _____

8. Dr. Levine *doesn't have to work* today.   _____

9. Alex *can't find* the maternity ward.   _____

10. Frank *shouldn't worry* so much.   _____

11. Clara *should try* to get more exercise.   _____

12. The noise in the wall *may be* a mouse.   _____

12. What else *could* the noise *be*?   _____

14. Barnie *can answer* the phones.   _____

15. *Could* John *help* us to push the car?   _____

EXERCISE 4

Circle and correct the errors in the following sentences.

1. Francine should has known better than to drink and drive. She is 40 years old!

2. I don't understand why a hockey player would earned such a big salary!

3. On the Internet you can send and received e-mail.

4. Your screenplay is good, but the movie should ended in a tragedy.

5. They held a tournament to discover who can slay the dragon.

6. When their sick mother fell asleep yesterday, the children should not made so much noise.

EXERCISE 5

Fill in the blanks using modals. Sometimes there may be more than one choice.

1. Paula has salty fingers that smell like vinegar. She (eat) _____ the salt and vinegar chips!

2. You (tell, not) _____ Celine about the party! It was supposed to be a surprise!

3. When I was younger, I (do) _____ one hundred sit-ups. Now I (do, not) _____ twenty of them.

4. Excuse me. (make, I) _____ an appointment to speak to Mr. Bindi, please?

5. I was caught driving without a seatbelt last month, and I (pay) _____ a big fine, so I went to City Hall yesterday to pay it.

6. I'm sorry, but I (leave) _____ now. I have no choice.

A conversation between a customer (C) and a store clerk (SC)

7. C: Excuse me, but (you, help) _____ me? I (find, not) _____ any writing paper.

8. SC: You (look) _____ in aisle 2, next to the pens and pencils.

9. C: I have looked there already. There isn't any unlined writing paper. I (buy) _____ *unlined* writing paper.

10. SC: Why (it, be) _____ be unlined?

11. C: Well, my teacher asked us to buy unlined paper. She told us that we (find) _____ it here.

12. SC: Well, your teacher (make) _____ a mistake! We never have unlined writing paper. You (try) _____ the store across the street.

Modals in the Passive Voice

Summary of Modals in the Passive Voice

Active	Passive
	modal + *be* + the past participle
Harold **should do** the job alone.	*The job **should be done** alone.*
People **must take off** their boots.	*Boots **must be taken off** at the door.*
Someone **can use** the phone now.	*The phone **can be used** now.*
The judge **ought to send** him to prison.	*He **ought to be sent** to prison.*
He **has to pay** the dentist.	*The dentist **has to be paid**.*

Note: For most past form modals, use modal + *have been* + past participle.
Jake must have eaten the pizza.   *The pizza must have been eaten.*

EXERCISE 6

Complete the passage using the active or passive form of the modal and verb. Be sure that you have used the correct tense.

1. Virtual reality is a new technology that lets you experience, in three dimensions, a simulated reality. Virtual reality (can, use) _____ by everybody. In my opinion the technology (should, use) _____ only for altruistic reasons. For example, in medicine the technology (could, enable) _____ surgeons to visualize complicated surgical procedures.

2. Unfortunately, this technology has already been used for morally questionable purposes. There is speculation that, in the past, some armies, (may, train) _____ their soldiers by using that technology.

3. Presently, this technology (can, incorporate) _____ into the training of soldiers in the several ways. The soldier (may, believe) _____ that he or she is shooting at a "virtual body," yet the body would look almost exactly like a real person. This (could, use) _____ as a method of desensitizing young soldiers.

CLASS EXERCISE

Fill in the blanks with the active or the passive form of the modal and verb. Be sure that you have used the correct tense.

Kara, my four-year-old sister (1. can, go, not) _____ outside yesterday. She (2. have to, stay) _____ in bed because she had a flu bug. She (3. can, not, get) _____ out of bed because she felt so weak. She also had a high fever. Her temperature (4. have to, take) _____ every four hours by my mother. Kara (5. can, not, give) _____ any solid foods. She (6. should, have) _____ some medicine to reduce her fever but she didn't want any. Last night, at about 10 p.m., she (7. have to, bring) _____ to the hospital by my father, because her fever was so high. She was so weak at that time that she (8. have to, carry) _____ into the hospital by my father.

8 Conditional Sentences

Conditional sentences have two parts. The main clause depends on the condition set in the *if* clause.

Main clause	*If* clause
Mary will help us	if we ask her.
Pedro would visit you	if you invited him.
Carolyn would have called	if she had had more time.

The problems with conditional sentences occur when we change the type of condition. If something is possible, the conditional form is easy to create. The type of sentence becomes more complicated when we talk about something that is not really probable, or about something in the past that is impossible.

Possible Future

In Possible Future sentences, the condition is something that will probably happen.

*If you **brush** your teeth after every meal, you **will get** fewer cavities.*

If & present tense ⟶ future tense

EXERCISE 1

Complete the sentences below. The following sentences express possible situations.

1. I have been working overtime lately. If my boss (give) _____ me a few days off, I will call you at your country house. If you need any groceries brought to the country house, just call me, and I (bring) _____ them to you.

2. If the weather (be) _____ nice next weekend, we will have a soccer practice. If it (rain) _____ , the practice (be) _____ canceled.

3. You (learn, not) _____ how to play the piano if you (practice, not) _____ . If you (try) _____ to play the scales every day, you (improve) _____ a lot.

Unlikely Present

In Unlikely Present sentences, the condition is something that is very improbable.

> *If I **won** a million dollars in the lottery, I **would buy** a new car.*
>
> *If I **won** a lot of money, I **could buy** a new house.*

The odds of winning the lottery are very remote. In these types of sentences, we simply express a wish about an unlikely situation.
Would expresses the intention to do something.
Could expresses the possibility of doing something.

In the *if* clause, the past verb tense is used. With the verb *be*, use the *were* form with all subjects. (In colloquial or "street" English, you occasionally hear *was*.)

> *If I **were** you, I **would stop** smoking.*
>
> *If she **were** a bit older, she **would behave** much better.*

> If & past tense ——→ would (stop / quit / find ...)
> were

EXERCISE 2

Complete the sentences below. Each sentence expresses an unlikely situation.

1. If I won a million dollars in the lottery, I (build) _____ myself a large house, and I (put) _____ a large art room on the top floor. The art room (have) _____ large windows on every wall.

2. Kira works long days at the factory, and she barely makes ends meet. Kira would visit us more often if she (have) _____ just a little more free time. Kira's boss is very unreasonable. If I (be) _____ Kira, I (look) _____ for another job.

3. Selvan says that he (fly) _____ to Sri Lanka if he had the money. Unfortunately, he doesn't have enough money right now. If I (be) _____ rich, I (give) _____ him a plane ticket so that he could visit his family.

CLASS EXERCISE

In each of the following sentences, decide whether the situation is possible or unlikely, and choose the correct form of the verb.

Possible Future: *If* & present tense ⟶ future tense	
Unlikely Present: *If* & past tense ⟶ would (stop / quit / find ...)	
were	

1. Errol really loves you. He will marry you if you just (ask) _____ him. I know he will. If I (be) _____ you, I would propose to him.

2. The band (play) _____ at the Spectrum for another night if they have time in their schedule. If it were possible, the crowd (ask) _____ that band to perform for 20 shows.

3. If Mrs. Lacombe were my mother, I (ask) _____ her for a really big allowance. I know that I can't ask my mother for more money. If my mother (have) _____ the money, I know that she would give it to me, but my mother (have, not) _____ extra money.

4. I'm looking for a job so that I can help my mother with expenses. If I (can) _____ work anywhere, I would work as a highly paid musician, but that's just a dream. In the real world, I think that Mr. Burger will hire me. If he (give) _____ me a job at his restaurant, I will buy groceries for my family, and if I (have) _____ extra money after that, I (pay) _____ for my university tuition.

Impossible Past

In Impossible Past sentences, the condition is something that cannot happen, because the event is over. The speaker expresses regret about a past event, or expresses the wish that a past event had worked out differently.

If I **had known** that he was dying, I **would have forgiven** him!

If you **had completed** your assignments, you **would have passed** the course.

> If & past perfect tense ⟶ would have (past participle)

CLASS EXERCISE

The following situations occurred, and cannot be changed. However, we can dream about changing the past. For each situation, write an impossible past conditional statement.

For example:

Mr. Tanguay won last fall's election because he promised to lower taxes. After the election he broke his promise.

If the politician had been honest, he would probably have lost the election.

1. Martin was supposed to graduate from high school in 1995, but he dropped out. He couldn't get a good job after that.

_____

2. Alfred was always faithful to his wife, but last December he found out that she had cheated on him. Alfred divorced his wife last March because of the affair.

_____

3. The students went on strike last week. The government threatened to raise tuition fees. The government would not promise to freeze tuition fees.

_____

4. Carolyn had a pneumonia last month, but she went to work anyway. Last week she was admitted to a hospital, and was forced to get some rest.

_____

5. Yesterday, Santiago ate lunch at an "all you can eat" restaurant. Yesterday afternoon Santiago felt ill, because he had overeaten.

_____

EXERCISE 3

Complete the conditional sentences below. Use the correct tense.

1. If Ellen inherits her father's money, she (invest) it in the stock market.   _____

2. If I inherited his money, I (save) it in a term deposit.   _____

3. If my late brother had inherited a lot of money, he (spend) it.   _____

4. Chris (wait) for you if you had asked him to.   _____

5. I (wait) for you if you want me to.   _____

6. Probably Jay (wait) for you if he didn't have to pick up his kids.   _____

7. My life (be) different if I had married Margaret.   _____

8. If you (be) nicer to people, you would have more friends.   _____

9. If I (be) nicer to people, I would have had more friends.   _____

10. We would have made more progress if we (work) together.   _____

11. We would make more progress if we (work) together.   _____

12. We will make more progress if we (work) together.   _____

Making a Wish

Wish about the Present

We make a wish when we want things to be different. When you wish about a present situation, use the past tense.

> *I wish I **knew** how to play the violin.*

> (I can't play the violin, but I would like to.)

With the verb *be*, always use the *were* form.

> *She wishes that she **were** thinner.*

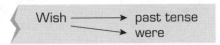

Wish about the Past

When you wish you could change a past situation, use the past perfect tense.

> *Yukio wishes that he **had told** the truth to his wife.*

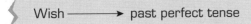

EXERCISE 4

Write the correct form of the verb in parentheses.

1. I wish I (stay) _____ in school when I was young. I'm 38, and I work in a restaurant. It's not a terrible job, but the salary is very low. If I (stay) _____ in school when I was a teenager, maybe I would have had an easier life. I wish I (think) _____ more about my future when I was a teenager.

2. Diego wishes he (understand) _____ English. He speaks Spanish, but he can't really communicate very well in English. He wishes that he (have) _____ the time to take a language course, but he can't because he works long hours.

3. Heather wishes that she (go) _____ to the show last night. She didn't come with us, and now she knows that the show was really fantastic.

4. Barry wishes that he (break up, not) _____ with his girlfriend last month. Now his girlfriend is dating someone else, and Barry misses her. He wishes that he (try) _____ harder to keep the relationship going. Now Barry feels lonely and he wishes that he (have) _____ a new girlfriend.

Conditionals Review

Possible Future: If & present tense ⟶ future tense

Unlikely Present: If & past tense ⟶ would* (go, eat …)
were ⟶

Impossible Past: If & past perfect tense ⟶ would have
(past participle)

Wish About the Present: Wish ⟶ past tense
were

Wish About the Past: Wish ⟶ past perfect tense

*Could, expressing possibility, can be used instead of would, which expresses intention.

CLASS EXERCISE: REVIEW

Complete the sentences below. Remember to use the correct tense.

1. If you (give) _____ me your telephone number, I will call you, and if I have the time later, I (visit) _____ you.

2. If Anna had a million dollars, she (spend) _____ the money in Las Vegas. She loves to go there. I hate gambling. If I had a million dollars, I (invest) _____ in real estate. I (buy) _____ a piece of land in the interior of British Columbia.

3. If you (see) _____ Rosa, will you tell her that I called. I really need to talk with her. I want to apologize to her. Yesterday, I was really rude to her. I wish I (be) _____ nicer to Rosa yesterday. If I (stop) _____ to think about her feelings, instead of just mouthing off, I would have realized that she was really upset by my comments.

4. Rick is so lazy. He never studies; he just spends hours playing video games. He failed his math test yesterday. If he (study) _____ , he (pass) _____ the test, but he didn't study at all. I keep telling Rick, "If you study, you (pass) _____ your tests!" I wish that Rick (listen) _____ to me more often.

5. I wish my mother (go) _____ to the dentist last year. Instead, she waited until her pain was unbearable, and yesterday she had an expensive root canal. If she (go) _____ to the dentist sooner, she could have avoided the costly procedure.

Combining and Punctuating Sentences

When you write in English now, it is important to use a variety of sentence types. Essays written entirely with simple sentences are fine when you are a beginning student in English, but now it is important to use more complex sentences. In the first part of this section, you will practice combining simple sentences to create more complex and interesting sentences.

Combining Sentences

Sentence Types

A *simple* sentence has one independent clause, or one complete idea.

> *The local team won the field hockey game.*

A *compound* sentence contains two or more complete ideas joined by a coordinating conjunction. You know a sentence is compound when you can cover the coordinating conjunction (*and, but, or, nor, for*) and still have two complete sentences.

> *Some apples were full of worms this season, **but** the strawberries were perfectly formed.*

A *complex* sentence contains one independent clause (complete idea) and one dependent clause (incomplete idea).

> dependent clause   independent clause
>
> ***Although some apples were full of worms**, I still refuse to spray the trees with pesticides.*

Although some apples were full of worms cannot stand alone even though it has a subject and a verb. The subordinator *although* turns this into a fragment, or part, of another sentence. Some other subordinators are *who, what, when, where, why, that, which, unless, because, in spite of, until.*

CLASS EXERCISE

A. On a piece of paper, practice making one compound sentence and one complex sentence out each group of sentences.

B. Combine each group of sentences into a single sentence.

Example: (A)   Last night I was very tired **but** I watched a program anyway. (compound)

I watched a program **that was on the CBC**. (complex)

1. a. Last night, I was very tired.
   b. I watched a program anyway.
   c. The program was called *Witness*.
   d. It was on the CBC.
   e. It was about Japan.
   f. The Japanese are interested in Canada.

2. a. There is a theme park in Japan.
   b. The park is called "Canada Land."
   c. There is an *Anne of Green Gables* exhibit in Canada Land.
   d. There is a replica of a Quebec City street in Canada Land.
   e. There are not exhibits about every part of Canada.

Sentence Hints

Combining sentences to make a clear sentence is not too difficult if you can avoid the following pitfalls:

1. Use *who* or *whom* to begin a clause only when you are adding information about a **person**.

*The young children, **whom I'd never seen before**, were making a lot of noise.*

2. When you are giving further information about a **place** or **thing**, use *which* or *that*.

*The series of articles **that I'm working on** should be ready soon.*

*The items **which were stolen** were in my purse.*

3. When you use interrupting phrases in a sentence, make sure that your subject still agrees with your verb.

*The **Fringe Festival**, which is located in Edmonton, **attracts** a lot of entertainers.*

EXERCISE 1

Combine the sentences with *who* or *that*. Sentences may be structured in more than one way.

1. _____

Maxine is an only child. She is very spoiled.

2. _____

The issues must be resolved. We discussed those issues.

3. _____

Long division can be very important. You learned long division in high school.

4. _____

Susan lives next door. She is a single mother.

5. _____

The plates are on the table. My grandmother gave me those plates.

Where in a clause is used to give more information about a place.

> The house is old and quaint. Kramer lives in the house.
>
> *The house **where Kramer lives** is old and quaint.*

Whose is used to indicate possession. It can replace *his, her, its* or *their*.

> I saw a dog. Its collar was missing.
>
> *I saw a dog **whose collar was missing.***

EXERCISE 2

Combine the sentences. Use *where* or *whose*.

Example: Did you see the two women. ̶T̶h̶e̶i̶r̶ (whose) dresses were identical.

1. The restaurant is understaffed. We ate in that restaurant this morning.

_____

2. Ralph saw a young, shy girl. Her date was very tall.

_____

3. That is the safe. I keep my valuables in that safe.

_____

4. The hospital has burned down. Kelly was born in that hospital.

_____

5. Did you notice that man? His tie is on crooked.

_____

6. The garage is expensive. My car was repaired in that garage.

_____

Sentence Construction Problems

Fragments and run-ons are two common errors students make when combining sentences.

A *fragment* is an incomplete sentence. Make sure that your sentence contains a complete thought.

> Fragment: *Because I really needed to see him.*
>
> Correct: *I was upset because I really needed to see him.*

A *run-on* occurs when two or more complete sentences are incorrectly connected.

> Run-on: *Maria missed the bus to work, she was extremely late.*

The above sentence could be corrected in the following ways:

1. Create two complete sentences   *Maria missed the bus to work. She was extremely late.*

2. Add a subordinator   **Because** *Maria missed the bus to work, she was extremely late.*

3. Add a coordinator   *Maria missed the bus to work* **and** *she was extremely late.*

4. Add a semicolon (;)   *Maria missed the bus to work; she was extremely late.*

EXERCISE 3

Identify all correct sentences with *C*. Write *F* beside fragments, and *RO* beside run-ons.

1. First, the best way to discipline children.

2. I think that children should not be hit. _____

3. That is a controversial topic, many talk shows discuss that issue. _____

4. I think that children can learn to distinguish right from wrong with a lecture, some disagree. _____

5. Because small children won't always understand explanations.

6. Some people believe that small children should be spanked if they do something wrong. _____

7. Small children understand that they are being bad when parents speak in a loud voice. _____

8. But not everyone can be convinced of that. _____

EXERCISE 4

Complete the dialogue by putting one of the following transition words in the spaces provided.

however	as soon as	therefore
although	as long as	furthermore
because	in spite of	besides

Dear Edwin,

(1) _____ I haven't written to you for quite some time, I have been thinking of you. (2) _____ I have some free time, I will come by your office and invite you for a drink. (3) _____ of my extremely busy workload, (4) _____ , I don't foresee having any extra time until next month. (5) _____ our busy schedules, we really should keep in touch more regularly. If we let our friends disappear, what will we do when we're old and retired?

I want to fill you in on my activities these days. The private eye business is going full steam. Right now I'm working on cases that require a lot of skill and patience. (6) _____ I can't tell you the details, I can give you some broad outlines of the cases I'm working on. Of course, I've got the requisite number of cheating spouse cases, but the most interesting investigation I'm doing is for a mysterious, beautiful lady. She comes in here and, (7) _____ the NO SMOKING signs everywhere, she smokes constantly, lighting one cigarette from the burning butt of another. She puts them out in a portable ashtray that she carries in her purse. (8) _____ , she drinks cup after cup from my espresso machine, yet (9) _____ all that stimulation, she talks with a slow, languid drawl, and moves with the laziness of a cat. I don't say a word about the smoking because she's too interesting to insult; (10) _____ , she's paying me a small fortune.

I can't say any more about this. I really have got a lot of work to do. Take care of yourself, and drop me a line.

Sincerely,

James Jameson

EXERCISE 5

Combine the following sentences into a single sentence. There may be more than one correct answer.

Malcolm entered the hotel room.

He put his briefcase on the desk.

Malcolm wanted to open his briefcase.

The briefcase was locked.

Malcolm didn't remember the combination for the lock.

Malcolm opened the case anyway.

He smashed the lock with a small hammer.

_____

_____

_____

_____

Punctuating Sentences

You have practiced combining sentences. Notice that there can be punctuation problems when you write longer sentences. Sentences that are incorrectly joined together can become run-on sentences. This part of Chapter 9 contains explanations for the proper use of the comma and the semicolon in English.

English as a Second Language students may also encounter problems with capitalizing. For example, days of the week are not capitalized in many Latin languages, but they are always capitalized in English.

Do the following exercises carefully so that you can learn to eliminate capitalization and sentence punctuation problems.

Capitalization

When to Use Capitals

Always capitalize the following:

1. The pronoun *I*.

2. The days of the week, the months, and holidays.

Tuesday   *May 22*   *Labour Day*

When to Use Capitals

3. The names of specific places, such as buildings, streets, parks, public squares, lakes, rivers, cities, provinces, and countries.

Elm Street	*Lake Louise*	*Regina, Saskatchewan*
Jarry Park	*St. Lawrence River*	*California*
Times Square	*Austria*	*Dylan Elementary School*

4. The names of languages, nationalities, tribes, races, and religions.

Norwegian	*Mohawk*	*Catholic*

5. The titles of specific individuals.

General Audet	*the Senator*	*Doctor Mortis*

If you are referring to the profession in general, do not use capitals.

a general	*senators*	*the doctors*

6. The major words in titles.

The Catcher in the Rye	*The Diviners*	*War and Peace*

EXERCISE 6

Add capitals, where needed, to the following sentences.

1. next monday we hope to visit castle mountain in banff national park, and in july we will go down the elbow river on an inner tube.

2. we asked the colonel if he was aware of the problems in the military, but he claimed that the sergeants hadn't told him a thing.

3. in ireland the catholics and the protestants have been fighting for over a century.

4. many presidents of major companies listened to president goldsmith's speech.

5. students at churchill high school can study latin, german and spanish as well as french, but other high school students in the area cannot.

Punctuating Titles

Place the title of a short work (song, essay, poem, short story, article from a magazine or newspaper) in quotation marks. (" ")

My brother used to listen to "Stairway to Heaven" every evening.

Underline the title of a longer work (book, TV show, play, movie, newspaper, magazine, or work of art) or use italics if you are typing a document.

Last summer, when we were in London, we saw the play <u>Evita</u>.

CLASS EXERCISE

Add capitals, where needed, to the following sentences, and properly punctuate titles. The first word of each sentence is already capitalized.

In may, my friend rita and i read east of eden. We are both avid readers, but she prefers reading short stories whereas I like long novels. Her favorite short story is called bugs, by nancy holmes. She also likes to go to the theater, and she enjoys reading plays. She wants me to read the play murder in the cathedral, by t.s. eliot. She said that the play takes place in a place called canterbury.

At the moment we are sitting by a river drinking a glass of iced tea and reading. The st. lawrence river is rushing by, and lake of two mountains isn't very far from here. I have a magazine with me today. I am going to read the article how to communicate in relationships, by doctor nancy wilder. I started to read the article on wednesday, but i haven't had time to finish it. Today rita just has a copy of the montreal gazette.

Using the Comma and the Semicolon

When to Use the Comma

Some uses of the comma are:

1. to separate items in a series of nouns, adverbs, verbs, or phrases. (A series = more than two.) Make sure that you put a comma before the final *and* or *or*.
We were impressed with her poise, her simplicity, and her kindness.
They shouldn't leave at this moment, in a day, or even in a week.

2. to set off phrases that give additional information about the noun.
Mr. Green, the man in the yellow trenchcoat, is a secret agent.

3. to set off introductory phrases such as *by the way, on the other hand, in the first place.*
On the other hand, we could cancel the meeting.

4. to signal that an introductory clause has ended. A clause is "introductory" if it begins with a subordinator (see list below).
*She worked very hard **in spite of** her poor health.* (No comma)
***In spite of** her poor health, she worked very hard.* (Comma)

Subordinators

Time clause	as soon as, as long as, when, whenever, while, since, until
Unexpected result	although, even though, despite, in spite of
Opposite clause	whereas
Clause of reason	because, due to, so, since (meaning "because"), as (meaning "because")

EXERCISE 7

When necessary, add commas to the following sentences.

1. Due to the poor visibility driving on the highway is not recommended.

2. You should know my friend that I have remarried my first wife.

3. We bought medical supplies including Band-Aids gauze peroxide antibacterial gel and tape.

4. I will jog every morning as long as I am able to.

5. Until you get a raise we should curb our spending.

When to Use the Semicolon

Use a semicolon:

1. when two sentences with complete ideas are joined together.

I think that bank machines are a necessity; my uncle refuses to use them.

2. when the second independent clause is introduced with a transitional expression like *therefore, however, furthermore, moreover, in fact* or *nevertheless*. Put a semicolon before, and a comma after, these transitional expressions when they introduce the second complete idea.

I showed my uncle how to use bank machines; nevertheless, he refuses to use them.

Our estimate for the work was very low; however, another company's bid was lower.

EXERCISE 8

Read the following sentences and correct any errors in punctuation, subject-verb agreement, or use of *who* and *that*.

Example: History is a subject who I adore. *"Who" is incorrect and should be replaced by "that."*

1. Young people who commits murder should be tried as adults.

2. Although I had never discussed the issue with my husband. I knew that he would support my decision.

3. Most humans believe in life after death, they want to believe that life has meaning.

4. The hockey league is a business who has been changed by million dollar salaries.

5. My teacher Mr. Steinberg loves to tell us stories about his youth.

6. Somebody removed the old suitcases that was under the bed.

7. Last month I read a really good article who said that ghosts exist.

8. Sales have fallen drastically, furthermore the company is in danger of becoming bankrupt.

9. That man, who is very nosey, always discuss my problems.

10. The game was canceled. Because of the bad weather.

CLASS EXERCISE

Read the following sentences and correct any errors in capitalization, punctuation, subject-verb agreement, or use of *who* and *that*.

1. *The White Hotel* is a novel who is greatly admired.

2. Although the story was very sad it was quite entertaining.

3. At that moment, Morgan and Alexandra, who was Arthur's half sisters, disappeared into thin air.

4. The police found the weapon who killed the old man.

5. The extinction of the dodo bird is a subject that interest me very much.

6. My cousin Arnie thinks that our grandmother is a nasty old lady, I think that granny is a sweetheart.

7. There are some interesting exhibits at the museum; and the entrance fee is very reasonable.

8. His new novel about some spies who evaded capture have become a bestseller.

9. Last week I saw a fantastic movie called voyage of the damned, it was about a terrible tragedy.

10. Because I am so busy I don't have time to work on that project with you.

11. The children don't have any winter boots, furthermore, we have run out of money.

12. Martin who is a member of the chess club, never wants to play chess with his younger sister.

13. On Tuesdays, my book-reading group gets together to discuss a novel, now we're discussing the novel, "wide sargasso sea," by Jean Rhys.

14. The Rocky mountains are incredible; and many people think that all tourists should visit them.

15. The Senators had to vote on the new bill, but I know of one Senator, Senator Gerard, who will vote against it.

10 Quotes and Reported Speech

Whenever you quote a passage, or even paraphrase an author's thoughts, it is extremely important to credit the author whose ideas you are using. Never present the words of someone else as if they were your own, or you could be accused of plagiarism.

When you write a formal paper containing a bibliography, you should refer to MLA rules for citing references. In more informal opinion essays, you do not need to include a bibliography, but it is extremely important to acknowledge the source of any material that you borrow.

Introducing and Punctuating a Quote

1. In informal essays, refer to the author and title in the sentence introducing or following the quote. After a complete introductory sentence, use a colon (:) followed by quotation marks (" ").

Dorothy Nixon, in her essay "The Appalling Truth," describes the effect of the telephone on modern humans: "The telephone has made us slaves, in the Pavlovian sense, to a ringing bell."

2. After an introductory phrase, use a comma followed by quotation marks.

In her essay "The Appalling Truth," Dorothy Nixon says, "The telephone has made us slaves, in the Pavlovian sense, to a ringing bell."

3. If the quote isn't a complete sentence but is integrated into your own sentence, no punctuation other than quotation marks is necessary.

Dorothy Nixon, in her essay "The Appalling Truth," claims that our phones have turned us into "slaves, in the Pavlovian sense, to a ringing bell."

4. The end punctuation of a quote is always placed inside the quotation marks.

   "What are you doing?" she asked.

   "The snails are superb!" he announced.

5. If the end of the quote isn't the end of your sentence, end the quote with a comma instead of a period.

   "With the invention of the clock we have lost the ability to live in the present," according to Dorothy Nixon.

6. Quotes of more than three lines in length should be indented and single spaced, and no quotation marks are necessary.

7. If you are quoting dialogue, begin a new paragraph each time the speaker changes.

EXERCISE 1

Punctuate the following sentences.

1. We really ought to leave now Rita muttered before he returns

2. Diego Parrera in his article in Sports Illustrated says An athlete is only as good as his or her last performance

3. Does anyone want to join me Tracy asked

4. According to Samuel Cleaver in his song An Odious Message the extinction of the dinosaurs contains a message for humans Who will study our bones when they end up in sandstone

5. Those convicted of drunk driving should lose their license for at least five years Marvin insisted.

   Gaby said That's a little harsh.

   That's because your father wasn't killed by a drunk driver Marvin responded loudly.

6. Various novels including The Catcher in the Rye are taught in high schools throughout North America.

Reported Speech

If you are a reporter working for a newspaper or magazine, you must report what someone said. Most newspaper articles do not contain a lot of direct quotes, but state what someone said indirectly. For example, a reporter might write: *The finance minister said that new ways must be found to reduce the deficit. He asked all of us to be partners in the government's new deficit-reducing schemes.*

Although it is interesting and useful to quote respected sources when you are writing an essay, it is also important to know how to properly report what reliable sources said. Notice the verb changes that occur when spoken words become reported words.

When we report a conversation after the fact, this is called *reported speech*. Because we are describing the conversation after it occurred, the past forms of verbs are generally used.

Quote	Reported Speech
Sara said, "I'm very busy."	*She said that she **was** very busy.*

Most verbs change to the past tense.

am / is ⟶ *was*   have ⟶ *had*

are ⟶ *were*   do ⟶ *did*

Change some modals in reported speech.

will ⟶ *would*

can ⟶ *could*

may ⟶ *might*

All other modals remain the same (*would, could, might, should, must, ought to*).

John: I should get ready for work.   *He said that he should get ready for work.*

The simple past can usually stay the same in reported speech, or you can change it to the past perfect.

Michele said, "I lost my keys." ⟶ *Michele said that she **lost** her keys.*

⟶ *Michele said that she **had lost** her keys.*

EXERCISE 2

Last Saturday you overheard this conversation. Report what was said by changing the following quotes to reported speech.

Quote	Reported Speech
Example: Roy: Tom is going to leave his wife.	Roy said (that) *Tom was going to leave his wife.*

1. Ann: Tom's wife will be devastated!   Ann said _____

_____

2. Roy: I know that.   Roy said _____

_____

3. Ann: Tom is a two-timer!   Ann said _____

_____

4. Roy: Tom is having a midlife crisis.   Roy said _____

_____

5. Ann: I can talk to Tom about it.

Ann said _____

_____

6. Roy: No, I will talk to him.

Roy said _____

_____

Other words change in reported speech.

Quote	Reported Speech
this	*that*
these	*those*
today	*that day*
now	*then*

EXERCISE 3

This dialogue was originally on the radio twenty years ago. Change the dialogue to reported speech.

Jay: I have an amazing new product. It is a hair restorer called Hair-In! Even if a man is completely bald, this product will restore some of his hair. Hair-In is made of rare plants from China. Many men will attest to the power of this product. If any listener is bald, and this product doesn't satisfy him, the money will be refunded. Hair-In costs only two dollars.

Jay said that he had an amazing new product. He said … _____

_____

_____

_____

_____

When to Use Say and Tell

Use *say*:

1. in direct quotations.

*Dimitrius **said**, "I am going to bed."*

2. in indirect (reported) quotations.

*Dimitrius **said** that he was going to bed.*
(*that* is optional)

Use *tell*:

1. when you give a message to somebody.

*Dimitrius **told me** that he was going to bed. Did he **tell you** that too?*

2. with the expressions *tell a lie, tell the truth, tell a secret.*

EXERCISE 4

Write *say* or *tell* in the spaces provided.

1. Last night Calvin _____ that he was going to bed but he really _____ a lie.

2. His parents _____ him to turn out his light and go to sleep.

3. They _____ that Calvin had been grumpy all day and they _____ that Calvin needed a good night's sleep.

4. Calvin _____ his parents that he would obey them, but instead he grabbed a book and a flashlight and he read under the covers.

5. In the morning, Calvin's parents _____ that he looked very tired.

6. Calvin _____ his parents that he had had a very bad dream.

7. When Calvin's mother _____ that she knew he had been reading during the night, Calvin _____ the truth to his parents.

Some terms can give a better indication of how something was stated than the word *said*.

state	mention	announce	offer
comment	reply	warn	remark
assure	insist	explain	admit

Compare: *Alex **said** that he had made a mistake.*

*Calvin **admitted** that he had made a mistake.*

CLASS EXERCISE

Look again at the text about Calvin. Try to replace *say* with any of the terms in the list above. (There are many possible choices.)

Reported Speech: Questions Form

You don't need to preserve the special question word order when the question is inside another, so the auxiliary after the question word is no longer necessary. However, you do need to change the present tense to the *past* tense.

       Auxiliary

What **do** you think about it?   *She asked me what I thought about it.*

If there is no question word, use *if* or *whether* to introduce the "inside" question.

Is it cold?   *He asked if it was cold.*

    He asked whether it was cold.

EXERCISE 5

Report what the customs inspector asked you yesterday.

Quote	Reported Speech
1. What is your name?	She asked me *what my name was*.
2. How are you?	She asked me
3. Do you have any alcohol or cigarettes?	She asked me
4. How long are you going to stay in Canada?	She asked me
5. Do you have any food in your bag?	She asked me
6. What gifts are you carrying?	She asked me
7. When will you leave the country?	She asked me
8. Can you open that bag please?	She asked me
9. Would you please follow that inspector?	She asked me
10. Do you have anything to declare?	She asked me

CLASS EXERCISE

Read the following conversation and then report what was said. Use the word in parentheses.

1. "I need some help," Jack said. (announce)

2. "A wolf is trying to eat me," Jack said. (explain)

3. "I see no wolf around here!" Mr. Ranger said. (comment)

4. "There really is no wolf. I just wanted to see someone," Jack said. (admit)

5. "Now I won't listen to any of your cries for help," Mr. Ranger said. (warn)

6. "I promise that I won't lie again!" Jack said. (assure)

Review of Chapters 6 to 10

CLASS EXERCISE A: PLURALS REVIEW

Add *s* to all nouns that require the plural form. For irregular plurals, rewrite the noun.

(1) My ideal man is a man who is sensitive, caring, witty, and clever. He has black hair and deep blue eye. He has cute foot and a nice behind. I'm really kidding about these physical aspect, though.

(2) Really, my ideal man is someone who cares a lot about his parent. I don't like man who are disrespectful to their elder.

(3) Finally, my ideal man is someone that most person like. If one of my friend hates this man, then he definitely isn't ideal!

CLASS EXERCISE B: MODALS REVIEW

Find and correct the modal errors in the following sentences. If the sentence is correct, write *C* in the space provided.

1. _____ I firmly believe that the age for getting a driver's license should be raise to eighteen.

2. _____ Many accidents could be avoid if only the young driver had more experience.

3. _____ Why he has to find a job?

4. _____ Mark should has known not to put the empty milk carton in the fridge!

5. _____ Sally shouldn't complain about her co-workers so much!

6. _____ When does the new law should be imposed?

7. _____ We think that the law should be implement as soon as possible.

8. _____ When you can help us to make the cookies?

9. _____ Where Margaret and I should meet you?

10. _____ Yesterday I shouldn't had worked late because I missed my daughter's
dance recital.

CLASS EXERCISE C: CONDITIONALS REVIEW

Complete the conditional sentences below.

If I can, I (give up) _____ smoking. I wish I (know)
_____ how to stop. I am pregnant, and I know that my
smoking could hurt my baby, but I'm totally addicted to cigarettes. I wish that I (never,
start) _____ smoking. I was so foolish. When I was 14, I just
tried smoking because I wanted to see what it felt like. If I hadn't bummed cigarettes
off of my friends, maybe I (become, not) _____ addicted. If I
(know) _____ , when I was 14, how hard it is to quit smoking,
maybe I (never, take) _____ that first puff.

CLASS EXERCISE D: PUNCTUATING SENTENCES REVIEW

Add proper punctuation and capitalization to the following sentences.

1. I don't have any particular religious belief moreover i don't think i'll ever be
religious even though my parents are devout catholics.

2. Every sunday morning i sit at home reading the calgary herald newspaper i only go
to church during the months of december and april.

3. I read an interesting article in the magazine called natural science the article was
called the human need for religious beliefs.

4. The article was written by a professor i think his name is professor santoni.

5. Because of the human need to believe that life has meaning virtually all cultures on
earth consider that there is some type of existence after death.

6. Next to some neanderthal skulls near the basin of the kroll river evidence of a
burial site was found stones were placed in a circle.

7. On the other hand the stone circle could have no significance in fact the stones
could have been placed near the skulls at a later date.

8. Although his colleagues disagree one individual professor santoni thinks that even
some apes have death rituals.

CLASS EXERCISE E: REPORTED SPEECH REVIEW

Change the quotes to reported speech.

	Quote	Reported Speech
1.	Could someone help me?	He asked if *someone could help him*
2.	Does anyone have the time?	He asked if
3.	Someone is at the door.	He mentioned that
4.	Can someone answer the door?	He asked if
5.	The neighbor needs some sugar.	He stated that
6.	There is no sugar left.	I replied that
7.	Will you buy some later?	He asked me if
8.	I won't have time to do it.	I answered that
9.	Does the corner store sell sugar?	He asked me if
10.	I can go to the store after lunch.	He explained that

CLASS EXERCISE F: QUOTATION MARKS REVIEW

Add quotation marks to the following text, or underline titles, when necessary.

Tracy Winland is a very efficient book editor. At the moment she is editing the cookbook One Hundred Chocolate Recipes. One summer morning she headed out for her usual coffee break.

Does anyone want to join me? she asked her co-workers.

No one did, so she went down the elevator to the ground floor of the building, and stopped at Lee's Newsstand, as usual.

A newspaper and a Boffo Chocobar please, she said. Tracy loves Boffo brand chocolate bars.

You really don't need to say a thing, Mr. Lee replied. I know that you always buy a newspaper and a Boffo Chocobar!

Once outside, Tracy sat on a long low wall. She was busy reading the article Health Matters in the Montreal Gazette when a handsome young man wearing a canary-yellow shirt sat on the wall next to her. The man was whistling the tune Over the Rainbow, and tucked under his elbow was a copy of Computer Magazine.

While Tracy was reading her article, the young man reached for the Boffo Chocobar on the ledge between them, broke off a large piece, and ate it. Tracy stared at the stranger. He hadn't even asked for a bite! Are you enjoying that? she inquired.

Oh yes, the young man replied, I certainly am. It's delicious.

To Tracy's horror the man then grabbed the bar, broke off another large piece, and ate that too. Barely a third of the chocolate bar was left. You've got some nerve, Tracy spit out, glaring into the man's surprised face. I'm going to finish this bar, if you don't mind!

At that, Tracy snatched the bar right out of the man's grasp, and stomped off. Some people are so rude! she called over her shoulder. On her way into the office building she ran into some co-workers, and she immediately told them about the chocolate bar thief. Everyone was very solicitous; they knew how much Tracy loved her chocolate.

As Tracy was walking through the lobby towards the elevator, Mr. Lee called out: Miss Winland! Come and get your Boffo Chocobar. You left it on my counter this morning!

11 Spelling

Because most languages have varieties of rules, and inconsistent pronunciation, spelling errors can and do occur. Even native English speakers make spelling mistakes.

Most of us have certain bad spelling habits. For example, some students constantly misspell the word *which* by writing *wich*. The best way to break a bad spelling habit is to keep a list of such spelling errors. Then, after you write a text, always reread your text specifically for spelling errors and consult your list to check that your habitual errors have not reoccurred. It is also very important to have a dictionary handy when you do a writing assignment.

If you are proficient on the computer, then you know that most computer programs have a spellcheck function. Be careful, however. Spellchecks can find some misspelled words, but not words that sound alike but differ in meaning. For example, a spellcheck would not find the mistakes in this sentence: *Your to late for the meeting at there house.*

EXERCISE 1

The following words are incorrectly spelled. Write down each word correctly.

Example:

tomorow   *tomorrow*

1. familly   _____

2. bussiness   _____

3. scool   _____

4. writting   _____

5. happenning   _____

6. embarassed   _____

7. sollution   _____

8. laught   _____

9. beggining   _____

10. writting   _____

CLASS EXERCISE

In the space provided: Write "f" if the *gh* sounds like *f*
Write "t" if the *ght* sounds like *t*
Write "silent" if the *gh* is silent.

1. rou*gh* _____

2. tau*ght* _____

3. borou*gh* _____

4. thou*ght* _____

5. lau*gh* _____

6. thorou*gh* _____

7. brou*ght* _____

8. cou*gh* _____

9. althou*gh* _____

10. slau*gh*ter _____

Spelling Tip 1: *Whose* and *Who's*

Whose indicates possession and replaces *his, her, its* or *their*.

Who's is the contracted form of *who is*.

EXERCISE 2

Choose the correct words from the lists provided.

1. (*his / is / has / as*)

_____ that Tom's desk? I need to leave this package on _____ desk.

_____ he in the building? _____ anyone seen him? _____ soon _____

he arrives, could someone let me know? _____ anyone listening to me?

2. (*whose / who's / live / leave*)

_____ cat is that? That cat's meowing is disturbing me!

_____ going to do something about it? Does that cat _____

with someone? How can I make the cat _____ this room?

3. (*your / you're*)

Is that _____ pen? I need to sign that letter. If _____ not using that

pen right now, could I borrow it, please?

4. (*their / there / they're*)

_____ are many people in this country who can't find work. I have two

unemployed uncles. _____ trying very hard to find jobs but _____

are no jobs available. Both uncles have lost _____ cars, and now they may

lose _____ homes because they can no longer pay the mortgages.

5. (*to / too / two*)

There are _____ reasons for me to stay at my job. There are perhaps several reasons why I should leave, _____ . If I go _____ another workplace, I may find myself with the same types of problems. It's really _____ difficult to make a decision now.

6. (*advise / advice*)

My sister Carol came to me for some _____ . She was thinking of entering an art program at the local university, instead of entering nursing. Unfortunately, I wasn't sure how to _____ her. If I suggested that she pursue art, maybe she wouldn't like my _____ , and if I suggested that she take the safer route and study nursing, maybe she would just ignore my _____ and study art anyway.

EXERCISE 3

These sentences each have one spelling mistake. Circle the spelling error in each sentence and write the word correctly in the space provided.

1. My father always gives me good advise. _____

2. Anne has been living alone for to long. _____

3. That wonderful new stereo over their is mine! _____

4. When my fly was open it was really embarassing. _____

5. Could you please ask John if he as seen Andy? _____

6. I though about it, but I don't want to do it. _____

7 I can't help you because I still have to much work to do. _____

8. Whose going to help me carry these boxes? _____

9. That is the man who's wife is in jail. _____

10. It is difficult to understand there reaction. _____

11. Martin is the type of person whose concerned about others. _____

12. Please do the work whit me. _____

13. I will make a thorough review of your case. _____

14. I would like to order an other coffee please. _____

15. The mariage of Sam and Rita will take place next Sunday. _____

EXERCISE 4

Spelling Tip 2: *IE* and *EI*

The following rhyme can help you remember when to write *ie* and when to write *ei*.
I before *E*, except after *C*, or when sounding like "ay" as in *neighbor* and *weigh*.

Which word is correctly spelled? Put A, B or C in the space provided.

1. A. deseive   B. deceive   C. decieve   _____

2. A. responsabillity   B. responsability   C. responsibility   _____

3. A. receive   B. recieve   C. resieve   _____

4. A. proove   B. prouve   C. prove   _____

5. A. exaggerate   B. exagerrate   C. exagerate   _____

6. A. believe   B. beleive   C. believ   _____

7. A. suceed   B. succede   C. succeed   _____

8. A. reciept   B. receipt   C. reseipt   _____

9. A. liscence   B. lisense   C. license   _____

10. A. freight train   B. frieght train   C. frate train   _____

EXERCISE 5

Choose the correct words from the list provided.

1. (*lose / loose / lost*)

I didn't _____ my snake ring. I gave it to my sister because it was too _____ for me. Unfortunately, I _____ my wedding ring at the mall.

2. (*we're / wear / where*)

_____ is Julie? _____ waiting for her. What does she want to _____ to the show?

3. (*proof / prove*)

I have no _____ that he committed the crime. Do you have any _____ ? Maybe no one can _____ it.

4. (*choose / choice / chose*)

What dress are you going to _____ for the wedding? Last week I _____ my dress, but I haven't paid for it yet. This store is great. It is difficult to make a _____ when there are so many dresses to _____ from.

5. (*then / than*)

I think that you are taller _____ I am, but _____ you would be, wouldn't you. You're much older _____ I am.

6. (*whether / weather / dessert / desert*)

I don't know _____ or not you are interested, but it is extremely hot outside. I can't stand this type of _____. I feel like we are living in the middle of the Gobi _____. Maybe I should have something cold, like a big bowl of ice cream, to cool off. I always like to eat _____ after supper.

Spelling Tip 3: Adding a Prefix or a Suffix

When you add a prefix (*un, pre, il,* etc.) to a word, keep the last letter of the prefix and the first letter of the base word.

> *un + necessary* = u**nn**ecessary (two *n*'s)

The same rule applies to the addition of a suffix. If you add *ly* to a word that ends in *l,* then your new word will have double *l.*

> *final + ly* = fina**ll**y (two *l*'s)

CLASS EXERCISE

These sentences each have one spelling mistake. Circle the mistake and write it correctly in the space provided.

1. Sherlock prooved that the butler murdered Mr. Lin. _____

2. I mispelled that word on my test. _____

3. I believe that there is an other way to solve the problem. _____

4. The banks are realy raising the service charges a lot this year. _____

5. I thing that handguns should not be sold. _____

6. Those are the books wich I want to borrow. _____

7. Drug smuggling is an ilegal activity. _____

8. You are acting in a very iresponsible way. _____

9. I didn't expect to like snails but actualy I enjoy them. _____

10. That is an iregular triangle. _____

11. Surelly you don't expect me to clean up that mess! _____

12. My teacher tought us to spell correctly. _____

12 Gallicisms

The English language of today has been influenced by many languages such as German, French, Greek, and the Scandinavian languages. The 11th-century invasion of Britain by the Norman French significantly transformed the English language. Because French was the language of British aristocracy and royalty for the next three centuries, French words permeated the English language, especially in the realms of law, finance, war, and royalty.

Because of the similarities in English and French, mistakes are easy to make. Some words sound the same but are spelled differently. Mistakes also occur when words look the same in both languages, but have completely different meanings.

EXERCISE 1

Write the English equivalent of each of the following French words. These words have the same meaning in both languages, but are spelled differently.

1.	adresse	_____	**11.**	juge	_____
2.	appartement	_____	**12.**	humain	_____
3.	canadien	_____	**13.**	langage	_____
4.	caractère	_____	**14.**	littérature	_____
5.	compagnie	_____	**15.**	personnalité	_____
6.	consécutif	_____	**16.**	potentiel	_____
7.	équipement	_____	**17.**	prouve	_____
8.	exemple	_____	**18.**	responsabilité	_____
9.	futur	_____	**19.**	recommandation	_____
10.	gouvernement	_____	**20.**	texte	_____

CLASS EXERCISE

The following English terms look like French words, but they do not have the same meaning in both languages. To verify that you understand what the following words mean in English, write an English synonym, or brief definition, for each term.

1a. actually _____   **1b.** presently _____

2a. sensible _____   **2b.** sensitive _____

3a. animator _____   **3b.** host _____

4a. formation _____   **4b.** background _____

5a. deception _____   **5b.** disappointment _____

6a. win _____   **6b.** earn _____

7a. vacancy _____   **7b.** vacation _____

8a. assist _____   **8b.** attend _____

EXERCISE 2

Sometimes French words or expressions are incorrectly translated. Correct the italicized word or phrase in each of the following sentences.

1. Alana was in a car accident, but don't worry. She is *correct*. _____

2. Arthur is addicted to the television. He *listens* the television every evening. _____

3. Your father thinks you should stay in school and I *am agree* with him. _____

4. Could you please *explain me* why I have to go to bed so early? _____

5. My mother was very *deceived* when I told her that I had failed my test. _____

6. Claude is the *animator* of a new television show. He interviews the guests. _____

7. Ron wants to quit his job because he only *wins* the minimum wage. _____

8. Marie *quit* her boyfriend because he was cheating on her. _____

9. Many terrible things have *arrived* since I last saw you. _____

10. Could you please *open* the radio? I want to listen to some music. _____

EXERCISE 3

Correct the translation error in each of the following sentences. (The incorrect word is in italics.)

1. Carl Sagan is a well-known *scientifique*, and he is the author of the book *Cosmos*. _____

2. Marie-Claire is going to do her teaching *stage* at the new high school. _____

3. Dr. Peablo has done some extremely interesting psychological *experiences*. _____

4. Terry has a *formation* in physics, but he is currently working as an astronomy teacher. _____

5. During my summer *vacancy* I went to Cape Cod, in the United States. _____

6. I really love Celine Dion, but I have never *assisted at* any of her concerts. _____

7. That movie is really *humoristic*. I laughed throughout the movie! _____

8. I like to *pass* my weekends at our cabin by the lake. _____

CLASS EXERCISE

Correct the translation error in each of the following sentences. (The incorrect word is in italics. The italicized word may have been incorrectly translated, or incorrectly spelled.)

1. I feel really *deceived* because I failed my math test. I really should have studied. _____

2. My father has two jobs because he doesn't *win* enough money with just one job. _____

3. Antoine rarely takes *responsability* for his actions. _____

4. Please *close* the lights when you leave the room. _____

5. During our summer *vacancy* we went to Newfoundland. _____

6. *Actually* I'm working as an accountant, but I hope to change jobs soon. _____

7. Greg has a perfect attendance record. So far this year he has *assisted at* all of his classes. _____

8. That young boy cries when he hears sad music because he is so *sensible*. _____

9. The lawyer is trying to *prouve* that his client is innocent. _____

10. How do you intend to *pass* your summer? _____

11. I'm sorry, but I can't discuss that with you. It's *personel*. _____

12. Octavio just got a job as the *animator* of a quiz show. _____

13. In order to get that job, you need a *formation* in computers. _____

14. Some people speculate that in the *futur* the middle class will disappear. _____

15. Martin *quit* work yesterday at midnight, and today he starts at 9 a.m. _____

Appendix 1

Parts of Speech

Knowing the parts of speech is useful when you need to edit a text. If you can recognize the type of error you may be better able to remember how to correct it.

Parts of Speech	
A	the article (*a*, *the*, ...)
N	the noun: a person, place or thing
V	the verb: the action word
Adv	the adverb: adds information about the verb (*typed* **rapidly**)
Adj	the adjective: adds information about the noun (**blue** *sky*)
P	the preposition (*in*, *on*, *at*, ...)
Pro	the pronoun (*I*, *me*, *my*, *mine*, *myself* ...)

CLASS EXERCISE

In the following sentences, identify the parts of speech. Leave blank any part of speech that you cannot identify.

          (N)   (V) (Pro) (Adj)   (N)   (P) (Pro) (N)

Example: Maria held her lovely rosary in her hand.

1. The nanny put the baby in its crib.

2. The blue documents are in the drawer of my desk.

3. The old man held the little dog gingerly.

4. The tiny bug bit the child on the leg.

5. Margaret carefully reads *People* magazine.

6. An efficient reporter asked his boss for a bonus.

7. She gently lifted the tired child.

8. The surprised woman politely thanked her cousin.

Appendix 2

Gerunds and Infinitives

1. Gerunds

A *gerund* is a verb in the *ing* form. Some verbs in English are always followed by a gerund. Do not confuse gerunds with progressive verb forms.
Notice the difference:

Nadia is sewing her dress.   ⟶   *Sewing* is in the present progressive form. Nadia is in the process of doing something.

*Frank finished **sewing** his pants.*   ⟶   *Sewing* is a gerund that follows *finish*. After *finish*, you must use a gerund. You cannot write "Frank finished to sew his pants."

Some Common Verbs Followed by Gerunds		
appreciate	enjoy	quit
avoid	finish	recall
complete	involve	recollect
consider	keep	regret
delay	mention	remember
deny	mind	resent
discuss	miss	resist
dislike	postpone	risk
practice	stop	

Gerunds are also used after the expressions *to be worth* and *no use*.

2. Infinitives

An *infinitive* is a verb in the *to* form. Some verbs in English are followed by the infinitive.

We can't afford **to buy** a new car. ⟶ After the word *afford* you must use the infinitive form. You cannot say "We can't afford buying a new car."

Some Common Verbs Followed by Infinitives

afford	demand	mean	seem
agree	deserve	need	threaten
appear	expect	prepare	volunteer
arrange	fail	pretend	want
ask	hesitate	promise	wish
claim	hope	refuse	would like
consent	learn	regret	struggle
decide	manage	plan	swear

3. Gerunds or Infinitives

Some verbs can be followed by either a gerund or an infinitive, and keep the same meaning.

Martin loves **to run** on the beach in bare feet. ⟶ Both sentences have exactly
Martin loves **running** on the beach in bare feet.   the same meaning.

Some Common Verbs Followed by Gerunds or Infinitives

start	like	prefer	begin	love
try	continue	hate	can't stand	

Some verbs can be followed by either a gerund or an infinitive, but there is a difference in meaning. Notice the difference in meaning:

I <u>stopped</u> **to have** a cigarette yesterday.	I stopped an activity to do something.
I <u>stopped</u> **smoking** yesterday.	I stopped doing something.
Did you <u>remember</u> **to turn** off the fan?	Did you remember to perform a task?
I <u>remember</u> **seeing** him at the crime scene.	I have a memory about something that happened in the past.

4. Prepositions Plus Gerunds

Many verbs have the structure verb + preposition + object. If the object is another verb, the second verb is a gerund.

*I'm excited **about travelling** to Greece.*

Certain verbs must have a noun or pronoun before the preposition.

Some Common Verbs Followed by Prepositions Plus Gerunds		
apologize for	fond of	look forward to
dream of	forgive **me** for	prevent **him** from
excited about	insist on	succeed in
feel like	interest in	think about

CLASS EXERCISE

Complete the sentence with the gerund or infinitive form of the verb. Simply write *to* before the verb or *ing* after it. In some instances, you may need to add a preposition before the gerund form.

Examples: Please forgive me **for (insult) ing** you.

Ovid appears eager **to (accept)** the deal.

1. My brother remembers   (hold)   me in his arms when I was a baby.

2. Please remember   (lock)   the doors when you leave.

3. We have finished   (make)   supper.

4. He is learning   (use)   a computer.

5. Mark is excited   (go)   to Florida.

6. Tony quit   (take)   drugs.

7. Be very careful. You don't want to risk   (catch)   a dangerous disease!

8. I like   (shop)   at that mall.

9. Would you mind   (help)   me lift this box?

10. You can't prevent her   (date)   that man.

11. I really miss   (spend)   time with my mother.

12. Jeremy's boss threatened   (fire)   him.

13. I promise   (rehire)   Jeremy.

14. My uncle is an alcoholic. He can't stop   (drink)

15. The students practiced   (pronounce)   the *r* sound.

16. My father is a handyman. He is used to   (work)   with his hands.

17. Do you really plan to stop   (bother)   him with those silly comments?

18. I really resent   (have)   to do almost all of the cleaning up around here.

19. She doesn't pretend   (speak)   Greek perfectly, but she does know enough to get by.

20. I don't think that his personality is worth   (discuss)   at this point.

21. I've arranged   (leave)   the keys with a neighbor.

22. My grandmother says that she has often regretted   (leave)   her homeland.

23. I'd like to apologize   (disturb)   your sleep.

24. Please stop   (stare)   at me. It makes me uncomfortable.

25. I'm thirsty. Could we stop   (buy)   a drink?

Appendix 3

Pronouns

Table of Pronouns

	Subject	Object	Possessive Adjective	Possessive Pronoun	Reflexive
Singular	I	me	my	mine	myself
	you	you	your	yours	yourself
	he	him	his	his	himself
	she	her	her	hers	herself
	it	it	its		itself
Plural	we	us	our	ours	ourselves
	you	you	your	yours	yourselves
	they	them	their	theirs	themselves

Rule 1: When the pronoun refers to the subject of the sentence, use the subject pronoun, and when it refers to the object of the sentence, use the object pronoun.

> *In spite of the difficulty, Mark and **I** climbed the mountain.*   (subject pronoun)
>
> *You really should excuse yourself to the Bensons and **me**.*   (object pronoun)

Rule 2: Sometimes a pronoun appears at the end of the sentence, and you're not sure if you should use the subject or the object pronoun. When in doubt, complete the thought.

> *She has worked here longer than **(I / me)**.*
> Complete the thought: *She has worked here longer than I have.*
>
> *The car belongs to Jane as much as **(I / me)**.*
> Complete the thought: *The car belongs to Jane as much as it belongs to me.*

Rule 3: Use *reflexive pronouns* when the subject doing the action and the object receiving the action are the same.

> *The Smiths should help **themselves** to the coffee.*
>
> *He is very proud of **himself**.*

CLASS EXERCISE

Circle the correct answer.

1. After I had insulted the hostess, I asked (me / myself) why I had been so rude.

2. Calvin has to help (him / himself) to dinner.

3. Ronald is Anna's son. Anna is (his / her) mother.

4. Marley is Bob's wife. Bob is (his / her) husband.

5. Sara has two sons. Those two boys are (his / her / hers).

6. The Langs are reclusive. They keep to (they / theirselves / themselves).

7. Little Billy cleaned his room by (him / hisself / himself).

8. He seems to be under the impression that he was smarter than (I / me), just because he received better marks in school than (I / me).

9. Anne bakes much better than (I / me).

10. We bought (us / ourselves) a dog.

11. When (your / you're) young, you don't have a lot of experience.

12. If (your / you're) going to walk there, wear a scarf.

13. Every worker should do (his or her / their) best.

14. It looks like (their / they're / there) going to be late again.

15. Anne asked us to visit, but Joe and (me / I) couldn't make it.

16. If you give us a lift, Marc and (I / me) would appreciate it.

17. Theresa helps everybody else more than (I / me).

18. Nobody talks as much as (she / her).

19. If you believe in (you / yourself) anything is possible.

20. Why didn't you ask (me / myself) to help you?

Appendix 4

Communication Activities

Grammar is more easily absorbed by students if they have an opportunity to integrate grammar into their activities. If the students have readings, they could be encouraged to discuss and debate the points in the readings. If the students are in a course that focuses on grammar, then the following activities can get the students to practice using the grammar.

The following activities could be used with students of all levels. For example, the first game appears easy, but even high-intermediate level students are unfamiliar with some of the verbs listed.

1. GESTURES GAME

(Present and past tenses)
The teacher chooses about 15 of the words. Students are then told to act out the words. The teacher may have to model each gesture once if the vocabulary is all unfamiliar for the students. Students who don't understand the vocabulary at the beginning of the game should understand it at the end of the game.

Suggested Vocabulary

wink	kiss	sip	tear	peel	put out	grab
blink	snore	swallow	sweep	scrub	take off	shove
shrug	snort	rub	wipe	scrape	put on	shovel
sob	cough	sneer	grind	spread	put down	turn on
sigh	sneeze	frown	mash	slice	pick up	turn off
laugh	clap	grin	sponge	chop	pick at	
giggle	tap	pout	stir	sprinkle	take away	
hug	snap	whine	spill	put away	dent	

Questions could also be practiced with this game. As one student acts out a verb, another could ask what he or she is doing, or did.

2. MYSTERY VERB GAME

(Present and past tenses, question forms)

The student must choose a word from the above list. For example, the student may decide to use the word *hug*. The other students must question the first student to try to find the mystery verb. All questions must be yes/no style questions. For example, the students in the class may ask the following types of questions:

Do you blank every morning?

Do you blank alone?

Do you blank in the kitchen?

Students use the word *blank* until they think that they have discovered the mystery verb. New verbs may be added to the list to make this game more challenging.

3. JOBS DISCUSSION

(Present, past and future tenses, modals)

Brainstorm a list of occupations on the board. Beside each occupation, list particular skills or qualities that are necessary for that type of job. Then, in a third column, write down the type of education that is needed for each job. Students can be encouraged to mention jobs that they have, or that their friends or family members have. Students can also think about their future ambitions, and their ideal jobs.

Example:

Occupation	Skills or Qualities	Education Needed
Doctor	Perseverance/Intelligence	University degree in medicine
	Ability to be emotionally detached	
	Ambition	
	Social skills (for effective interaction with patients)	

If the students have quite advanced vocabulary, find some more obscure jobs. For example: Primatologist, endocrinologist, etc.

Discuss which jobs are most likely to disappear in an increasingly computerized work place. Which jobs are probably the most stressful? Which jobs would be most difficult to combine with a family life?

4. RECREATE THE POSE

(Modals, imperatives)

Two students come to the front of the classroom and sit on chairs facing the same direction. Student A sits in front of Student B and cannot see Student B. Student B strikes, or is given, a relatively difficult pose. The students in the class must then give Student A directions so that he or she is in exactly the same pose as Student B. Students in the class are not allowed to indicate, with gestures, what the pose is. They must use language to describe the position of Student B.

5. TELL THE TRUTH

(All verb tenses, question forms)

Students must think up three stories about themselves. Two of the stories are true, and one is a lie. The other students must ask the first student very detailed questions to find out which story is the lie. Students must be very careful in their use of tenses, and the teacher should intervene if a student incorrectly forms a question. This activity should be modelled by the teacher first.

To encourage the students to participate, they could be given a point for each correct question. Therefore those who don't participate would get no points.

For example:

I was an extra in a Paul Newman movie in 1985. (lie)

I accidentally dropped a dictionary on my pet hamster when I was young. (true)

I won $50 in a lottery last week. (true)

Possible questions:

What is the name of the movie that you were in?

How many hamsters have you owned in your life?

Where did you buy last week's winning lottery ticket?

6. ROLE PLAYING SUGGESTIONS

One student should read a situation described below under the heading "Student A." The student's partner should read the same-numbered situation described under the heading "Student B." Both students then meet at the front of the class and role-play the situation.

Student A

1. You are interviewing a candidate for a job as a legal secretary. Ask the candidate about his or her salary requirements, family situation, reasons for wanting this job, skills, weaknesses and strengths, teamwork experience, and work experience. Be careful when you form questions. Make sure that you use the correct question word order. Because the job requires a lot of late hours, find out if the candidate can do overtime work.

2. You repair refrigerators. You come to fix someone's fridge. You very quickly change a small piece. The cost is $90. Be inflexible.

3. You are driving very quickly. When you are stopped for speeding, try to bribe the police officer.

4. You are sitting in an airplane. The passenger in front of you is smoking. Ask the passenger to stop smoking. You are asthmatic, and smoke is very bad for your health.

5. You are a teacher and your spouse is a lawyer. Your spouse has been offered a great job in Yellowknife. You don't want to go for many reasons.

6. You and your roommate found a mouse in the kitchen, and there is scratching behind the walls. You have also seen cockroaches in the kitchen. Explain the situation to the landlord. You would like the rent reduced because of these problems.

7. You go to the doctor. You often feel nauseous, and you have a headache and a sore throat. The doctor will explain what your ailment is. Refuse to take any antibiotics. Ask the doctor if he or she could suggest a homeopathic remedy, or a herbal tea. You don't believe in antibiotics.

8. Phone your child. You are 70 years old, and are not feeling very well. Your knees hurt, and lately you have been feeling faint. You are also very worried about your child's marriage. Lately your child has seemed very tense around his or her spouse, and they argue a lot. Try to get your child to talk about it. You are also upset because your grandchildren seem too thin. Maybe they aren't being fed enough. Make sure your child listens to you. After all, you went through 20 hours of labour to have that child!

Student B

1. You are being interviewed for a job as a legal secretary. Answer the interviewer's questions honestly. You really need this job because you are an unemployed single parent of three small children.

2. Your fridge doesn't defrost. A repair person comes to your door. The repair is done very quickly. You refuse to pay the bill because it is too high.

3. You are a police officer. Stop a motorist for speeding. Ask to see the motorist's identification papers.

4. You are in an airplane. You are enjoying a cigarette. When someone asks you to put it out, refuse. After all, the No Smoking light has been put out, and you are sitting in the smoking section.

5. You are a lawyer and your spouse is a teacher. You have just been offered a great job in Yellowknife, with a very high salary and very challenging work. You desperately want to go. You are bored and unmotivated in your present job, and really need the change. Convince your spouse to make the move.

6. You are the landlord of a very nice building. Two messy tenants make rather dubious complaints about their apartment. They are probably just trying to take advantage of your kind nature. Be firm with them. The other tenants in the building never have problems. Don't let these tenants get away with anything.

7. You are a doctor. Listen to a patient's complaints. After listening to the complaints, take a throat swab. The patient has severe strep throat and must go on antibiotics immediately. The infection could get much more serious without proper treatment, so make sure that the patient takes your advice. Write out a prescription.

8. Your mother calls. You feel quite tired after a long day of work, and you really just want to relax for a few minutes and read the newspaper before the kids get home from school. Soon you and your spouse have to prepare the evening meal. Be polite to your mother, but do let her know that you can't talk for long.

Appendix 5

Table of Irregular Verbs

Base Form	Simple Past	Past Participle	Base Form	Simple Past	Past Participle
Arise	Arose	Arisen	Do	Did	Done
Be	Was, were	Been	Draw	Drew	Drawn
Bear	Bore	Borne	Drink	Drank	Drunk
Beat	Beat	Beaten	Drive	Drove	Driven
Become	Became	Become	Eat	Ate	Eaten
Begin	Began	Begun	Fall	Fell	Fallen
Bend	Bent	Bent	Feed	Fed	Fed
Bet	Bet	Bet	Fight	Fought	Fought
Bind	Bound	Bound	Find	Found	Found
Bite	Bit	Bitten	Flee	Fled	Fled
Bleed	Bled	Bled	Fly	Flew	Flown
Blow	Blew	Blown	Forbid	Forbade	Forbidden
Break	Broke	Broken	Forget	Forgot	Forgotten
Bring	Brought	Brought	Forgive	Forgave	Forgiven
Build	Built	Built	Forsake	Forsook	Forsaken
Burst	Burst	Burst	Freeze	Froze	Frozen
Buy	Bought	Bought	Get	Got	Got, gotten
Catch	Caught	Caught	Give	Gave	Given
Choose	Chose	Chosen	Go	Went	Gone
Cling	Clung	Clung	Grind	Ground	Ground
Come	Came	Come	Grow	Grew	Grown
Cost	Cost	Cost	Hang	Hung	Hung
Creep	Crept	Crept	Have	Had	Had
Cut	Cut	Cut	Hear	Heard	Heard
Dig	Dug	Dug	Hide	Hid	Hidden

Base Form	Simple Past	Past Participle	Base Form	Simple Past	Past Participle
Hit	Hit	Hit	Sing	Sang	Sung
Hold	Held	Held	Sink	Sank	Sunk
Hurt	Hurt	Hurt	Sit	Sat	Sat
Keep	Kept	Kept	Sleep	Slept	Slept
Know	Knew	Known	Slide	Slid	Slid
Lay	Laid	Laid	Speak	Spoke	Spoken
Lead	Led	Led	Speed	Sped	Sped
Leave	Left	Left	Spend	Spent	Spent
Lend	Lent	Lent	Spin	Spun	Spun
Let	Let	Let	Split	Split	Split
Lie	Lay	Lain	Spread	Spread	Spread
Light	Lit	Lit	Spring	Sprang	Sprung
Lose	Lost	Lost	Stand	Stood	Stood
Make	Made	Made	Steal	Stole	Stolen
Mean	Meant	Meant	Stick	Stuck	Stuck
Meet	Met	Met	Sting	Stung	Stung
Pay	Paid	Paid	Stink	Stank	Stunk
Prove	Proved	Proved/Proven	Strike	Struck	Struck
Put	Put	Put	Swear	Swore	Sworn
Quit	Quit	Quit	Sweep	Swept	Swept
Read	Read	Read	Swim	Swam	Swum
Rid	Rid	Rid	Swing	Swung	Swung
Ride	Rode	Ridden	Take	Took	Taken
Ring	Rang	Rung	Teach	Taught	Taught
Rise	Rose	Risen	Tear	Tore	Torn
Run	Ran	Run	Tell	Told	Told
Say	Said	Said	Think	Thought	Thought
See	Saw	Seen	Throw	Threw	Thrown
Sell	Sold	Sold	Thrust	Thrust	Thrust
Send	Sent	Sent	Understand	Understood	Understood
Set	Set	Set	Upset	Upset	Upset
Shake	Shook	Shaken	Wake	Woke	Woken
Shine	Shone	Shone	Wear	Wore	Worn
Shoot	Shot	Shot	Weep	Wept	Wept
Show	Showed	Shown	Win	Won	Won
Shrink	Shrank	Shrunk	Wind	Wound	Wound
Shut	Shut	Shut	Withdraw	Withdrew	Withdrawn

Index